Classic Dishes of Decades Past

the cookbook of nostalgic house favorites

W9-BSE-385

Lou Seibert Pappas

illustrations by Shanti L. Nelson

Bristol Publishing Enterprises, Inc.
San Leandro, California

Printed in Korea through Spectrum Pte. Ltd

ISBN 1-55867-235-4

Design & Illustration by *Shanti L. Nelson*

Dedication

To the many friends who have graced my table
and enriched my life–thank you!

table of contents

Classic Dishes of Decades Past

Introduction

As the new millennium unfurls, recreating the nostalgic dishes of past decades is a joyful pursuit and a great way to retain the house favorites.

This collection of more than 100 dishes showcases long-time specialties and some newer classics. Some are unaltered from the past; others have timely updates to please today's palates. The extensive availability of worldly produce, fresh herbs, new condiments and other ingredients makes many recipes more tantalizing today. Also, seasonings have been expanded and refined from earlier eras.

Food has been my passion for my entire life. My love for fresh ingredients and delicious dining was nurtured as a child, growing up in the verdant Willamette Valley in Oregon. My father was a wholesale grocer for the University. Daily he brought home the freshest from the marketplace—King salmon, Dungeness crab, fresh asparagus, Tillamook cheddar cheese, raspberries and Bing cherries. My mother, of Swedish heritage, was a Northwest cook and superb baker. With a commercial mixer on the yellow tile counter, she turned out whole-grain breads and sticky cinnamon rolls, fresh-squeezed orange juice and an ever-changing repertoire of delectable desserts—prize sponge cake, special lemon pies, hazelnut tortes, wild blackberry and huckleberry tarts and whipped cream chocolate rolls.

Since the fifties

I have made California my home and have raised three sons and a daughter. I grow more than a dozen kinds of herbs and have as many fruit trees—navel orange, tangerine, blood orange, lemon, persimmon, white peach, apricot, Fuji apple, Granny Smith apple and Comice, Red Bartlett and Anjou pear. Plus, a strawberry patch flourishes from April to November.

I have enjoyed a fascinating career as a home economist with *Sunset* magazine and as food editor of the *Palo Alto Peninsula Times Tribune*. Food styling, producing articles for national magazines, and writing over 30 cookbooks dovetailed throughout this time frame. Today I teach participation-style cooking classes and write for the Internet.

With camera and notebook in hand, I have made over 50 trips abroad collecting recipes, and have met and traveled with many international culinary professionals. I am especially fond of Mediterranean cooking from the Provence region of France, Italy, Turkey and Greece.

Looking back decades

to the forties and fifties, I remember birthday parties savoring root beer floats, hamburgers, and chocolate fudge layer cake swirled with seven-minute frosting. Caesar and Cobb Salads were tearoom fare of that day; today they are reviving with prominence. Tabbouleh introduced what was then called "foreign food." Les Halles onion soup, lasagne and moussaka followed as continental discoveries.

As a young career girl and home economist at the West Coast *Sunset* magazine, I delved into worldly ethnic cooking. Marrying into a Greek family, I pursued this Mediterranean cuisine. Papa, my father-in-law, had owned a candy shop and ice cream fountain in San Francisco on Market Street just after the 1906 earthquake, and he indulged our young family with Greek specialties, ice cream sodas, apple pies and fudge. My mother-in-law inspired my first cookbook on Greek cooking.

Cooking and baking have always been a great pleasure and everyday pastime for me. I love to bake bread with interesting grains and nut flours, churn sorbets and ice creams and dash to the kitchen garden to pluck fresh herbs for the dish in the making.

Good cooking revolves around choosing the freshest prime ingredients and preparing them deftly with a minimum of complimentary seasonings. That is my philosophy for the recipes that follow. I hope you enjoy this worldly collection of house favorites to bridge the millennium.

Lou Seibert Pappas
Palo Alto, California
Fall 1999

Appetizers

Classic Dishes of Decades Past

Apricot- and Pistachio-Crowned Brie

Ever since I came to California in the fifties, I have indulged in fresh apricots in season. For the past twenty years in my garden, a prolific Blenheim apricot tree bursts forth with fruit every Fourth of July. It is always a challenge to save some juicy' cots for winter, either by sun-drying them or preserving them as fruit butter. Here is a favorite apricot indulgence as an appetizer. A wheel or of Brie gets a dressy fruit and nut topping for fast party fare.

1 wheel Brie cheese, about 1 pound
2 tablespoons orange curaçao,
   Cointreau, cognac or brandy
⅓ cup ¼-inch strips dried apricots
3 tablespoons golden raisins

3 tablespoons coarsely chopped
   pistachio nuts or pine nuts
1 loaf French-style baguette, cut into
   ⅓-inch-thick slices, or crackers

Preheat the oven to 350°. Place the Brie on an ovenproof serving platter. With a fork, prick the top of the Brie in a dozen places and drizzle with ½ tablespoon of the liqueur.

In a bowl, toss the remaining 1½ tablespoons of the liqueur with the apricots, raisins and pistachios and sprinkle the mixture over the top of the cheese.

Bake for 8 to 10 minutes, or just until the cheese warms and softens. Serve with the sliced bread or crackers.

Makes 12 Servings

Appetizers

Savory Cheese Triangles

These delectable savory pastries were an early taste treat after marrying into a Greek family in the fifties. Yaya, my mother-in-law, taught me the various folds for phyllo and I became fascinated with incorporating it into my recipe repertoire. Once you acquire the knack of working with this versatile dough, it becomes a staple for encasing many creations. Assemble the pastries in advance and freeze them, if desired, ready to bake just before guests arrive.

½ pound feta cheese
½ pound ricotta cheese
½ cup freshly grated Romano or Parmesan cheese
¾ cup shredded Gruyère or Samsoe cheese
2 tablespoons minced fresh flat-leaf parsley

2 tablespoons minced fresh chives
1 egg
1 egg yolk
⅛ teaspoon freshly ground nutmeg
½ pound (about 10 sheets) phyllo dough (see *Note*)
6 tablespoons unsalted butter, melted

Preheat the oven to 375°. In a mixer bowl or food processor workbowl, combine the cheeses, parsley and chives and mix or process until blended. Add the egg, egg yolk and nutmeg and mix well.

On a work surface, lay out the phyllo, one sheet at a time, and cut each sheet into 3-inch-wide strips about 12 inches long. (Keep the remaining phyllo covered with plastic wrap to prevent it from drying out.) Brush each strip lightly with melted butter. Place a rounded teaspoonful of the cheese mixture on one corner of each strip; fold the corner over to make a triangle. Continue folding the filo over in triangles, as if you are folding a flag. (If desired, you can freeze the triangles at this point; let them thaw before baking.) Place the packets seam-side down on a baking sheet. Repeat the cutting, brushing and filling process until all the ingredients are used. Bake the packets for 15 minutes, or until golden brown. Serve hot.

Note: If the phyllo dough is very thin, use 2 sheets, placed on top of each other and buttered lightly between them.

Makes 5 Dozen Triangles

Appetizers

West Coast Lavosh Roll

The crackly bread, lavosh, was an addictive discovery in the fifties when I first dined at the Armenian restaurant in San Francisco called Omar Khyam. More recently I have enjoyed it as a wrapper—dampened, stuffed and rolled to form a colorful pinwheel when sliced.

1 large round lavosh
8 ounces whipped light-style or regular cream cheese
1 teaspoon Dijon-style mustard
5 ounces thinly sliced smoked or flaked baked salmon, or thinly sliced smoked chicken or turkey breast

2 medium tomatoes, sliced as thinly as possible
½ cup fresh basil leaves
Thinly sliced cucumber (optional)
Outer leaves from 1 head romaine lettuce, center ribs removed
Chopped fresh chives to taste

Dampen one large or two smaller kitchen towels and wring out the excess moisture. Moisten the lavosh well on both sides under cold running water. Place the lavosh darker-side down between layers of the damp towel and let stand until soft and pliable, about 45 minutes. Remove the top towel.

In a bowl, mix the cream cheese and the mustard and spread over the surface of the lavosh. Top with the salmon or chicken. Top with the tomatoes, basil, cucumber, if using, and lettuce, stopping about 4 inches from the far edge. Sprinkle with the chives. Using the bottom towel to lift, fold an inch or so of the near edge of the lavosh over the filling and continue to roll, gently but firmly, jelly roll-fashion. Cover the roll securely with plastic wrap and chill for at least 1 hour or up to 24 hours. To serve, cut the roll crosswise into ¾-inch slices.

Note: Avocado also makes a good filling, replacing the salmon or chicken. Or create an all-vegetarian filling with grated carrot, sliced cucumber, alfalfa sprouts and diced artichoke hearts.

Makes 16 Slices

Appetizers

Gorgonzola Dip with Vegetables

In the eighties as fitness swept into style, I commenced making my own yogurt from one-percent milk, creating a quart at a time for smoothies, toppings and dips. Here yogurt enhances a zestful, light-style dip, sparked with pungent blue cheese. The dip achieves a versatile role for both raw and cooked vegetables. It does wonders to a baked potato or plate of sliced tomatoes. For a first course, I like to spoon it into small stoneware dishes or soufflé molds to make charming individual servings to accompany a plate of raw mushrooms, fennel and red and gold cherry tomatoes. Or, I place it in a bowl inside a head of curly red kale for a handsome look.

1 shallot, chopped
2 tablespoons chopped fresh flat-leaf parsley
2 tablespoons chopped fresh chives
2 teaspoons chopped fresh thyme or tarragon, or ½ teaspoon dried
1 cup (4 ounces) large-curd cottage cheese

½ cup plain yogurt
1 tablespoon balsamic vinegar
2 to 3 ounces Gorgonzola or other blue-veined cheese, crumbled
Raw vegetables or hot baked potatoes for accompaniments

In the workbowl of a food processor, place the shallot, parsley, chives, thyme or tarragon, cottage cheese, yogurt and vinegar and process until smooth. Add the Gorgonzola and process for a few seconds to mix.

Transfer the mixture to a serving container and chill until serving time. Serve with a basket or platter of raw vegetables or hot baked potatoes.

Makes 2 Cups

Herb-Cheese Soufflé

My early adventures with making a cheese soufflé involved first cooking a white sauce, a task I happily bypass once I discovered this method. Now I simply whisk together the cream cheese and yogurt for a base instead. I serve the soufflé as a first course with a salad of baby greens or garden arugula for a Sunday brunch or late supper. The soufflé can be assembled in advance and chilled to bake several hours later.

Butter and grated Parmesan cheese
   for coating dish
8 ounces light-style cream cheese or
   creamy goat cheese
⅓ cup plain yogurt or light-style
   sour cream
6 eggs, separated
2 tablespoons minced fresh chives
2 tablespoons minced fresh flat-leaf
   parsley

1½ teaspoons minced fresh tarragon,
   or ½ teaspoon dried
½ teaspoon salt
1 teaspoon Dijon-style mustard
¼ teaspoon freshly ground nutmeg
¼ teaspoon white pepper
1 cup shredded sharp cheddar
   or Gruyère cheese
¼ teaspoon cream of tartar

Preheat the oven to 400°. Butter a 10-inch round baking dish, 10-inch skillet or 1½-quart soufflé dish and coat with grated cheese.

In a large bowl, mix the cream cheese or goat cheese until light and fluffy. Add the yogurt or sour cream, egg yolks, chives, parsley, tarragon, salt, mustard, nutmeg and pepper and mix well. Stir in the shredded cheese.

In a large, clean, oil-free bowl, beat the egg whites until foamy. Add the cream of tartar and beat until stiff peaks form, but the mixture is not dry. Fold ¼ of the beaten egg whites into the cheese mixture to lighten it. Add the remaining egg whites to the lightened mixture and gently fold together until the ingredients are incorporated.

Transfer the mixture to the cheese-coated dish and smooth the top. Bake for 25 to 30 minutes, or until the center is set and the top is puffed and golden brown. Serve immediately.

Makes 6 Servings

Appetizers

Endive with Scallops or Shrimp

In the nineties, I toured the endive production farms in Belgium and learned the complex growing pattern of this regal vegetable; ever since, it has fascinated me and found a place in my culinary repertoire. Now endive is produced in California and is readily available in the market. I utilize both red and green endive stalks to form a piquant backdrop for curried seafood.

2 heads Belgian endive (red and green preferred)
¾ teaspoon curry powder
⅓ cup mayonnaise or sour cream

⅓ pound small scallops or small cooked shrimp
1 tablespoon butter

Separate the endive heads into single leaves.

Place the curry powder in a bowl and microwave on high (100%) for about 30 seconds to remove the raw taste. Add the mayonnaise or sour cream to the bowl and mix well. In a large skillet over medium-high heat, sauté the scallops in the butter, turning to brown both sides; cool.

To serve, place about ½ teaspoon of the mayonnaise or sour cream mixture on the end of each endive leaf and top with a scallop or 2 or 3 shrimp. Arrange the leaves on a platter in a decorative sunburst pattern.

Makes 20 Pieces

Appetizers

Pistachio Cheese Puffs

At a cocktail party in the Parisian apartment of cookbook author Patricia Wells, these golden cheese puffs, called *gougere*, starred alone with herb-scented olives and kir aperitifs. I like to top the appetizers with pistachios and serve them also as a hot bread to accompany a soup or salad supper. Extras can go in the freezer for last-minute snacks.

5 tablespoons butter
1 cup milk
¼ teaspoon salt
¼ teaspoon dry mustard
1 cup all-purpose flour

4 eggs
1 cup shredded Gruyère, smoked
    Gouda, Jarlsberg or Samsoe cheese
¼ cup chopped pistachio nuts, slivered
    blanched almonds or pine nuts

Preheat the oven to 375°. In a saucepan, heat the butter, milk, salt and mustard and bring to a rolling boil. Add the flour all at once and beat constantly with a wooden spoon over medium heat until the mixture leaves the sides of the pan and forms a ball. Remove from the heat. Add the eggs one at a time, beating until smooth. Add the cheese and beat well.

Place tablespoonfuls of dough in small mounds 2 inches apart on a parchment-lined or buttered baking sheet. Sprinkle with the nuts. Bake the puffs for 25 to 30 minutes, or until golden brown. Serve hot.

Makes 24 Puffs

Appetizers

Leek, Green Onion and Spinach Frittata Squares

For decades it seems, I've been whipping up these eggy spinach squares for appetizers. To boost the flavor, I recently added sweet caramelized leeks. If you are in a rush, one package of frozen chopped spinach, thawed and squeezed dry, can substitute for the fresh. These treats are good hot or cold.

2 bunches green onions, finely chopped
1 medium leek (white part only), chopped
1 tablespoon olive oil
1 bunch spinach, finely chopped
¼ cup minced fresh flat-leaf parsley
2 tablespoons minced fresh basil (optional)

Salt and freshly ground black pepper to taste
6 eggs
⅓ cup plain yogurt or light-style sour cream
1½ cups shredded Jarlsberg or sharp cheddar cheese
¼ cup freshly grated Parmesan cheese

Preheat the oven to 350°. In a large skillet, sauté the onions and leek in the oil over medium heat until soft and glazed. Add the spinach and sauté for 1 minute. Remove the skillet from the heat and add the parsley, basil, if using, salt and pepper; mix well and set aside.

In a large bowl, beat the eggs. Add the yogurt or sour cream, the shredded cheese and the vegetable mixture and mix well. Pour the egg mixture into an oiled 9-inch baking pan and sprinkle with the Parmesan cheese. Bake for 25 minutes, or until the eggs are set. Cut into squares and serve warm.

Makes 36 Squares

Mushroom and Red Onion Frittata Squares

Each autumn the past few years, I've tucked dozens of little red onion bulbs or sets into the ground. Come spring, their green tops are handy for mincing for garnishes and the little, sweet bulbs are good for dicing. Paired with wonderful full-flavored portobello mushrooms, the garden red onions enhance these custardy frittata squares.

1 medium-sized red onion, chopped
1 tablespoon olive oil
1 large portobello mushroom cap, chopped
¼ cup minced fresh flat-leaf parsley
3 tablespoons minced fresh basil
Salt and freshly ground black pepper to taste

6 eggs
⅓ cup plain yogurt or light-style sour cream
3 ounces prosciutto or ham, diced
1½ cups shredded Gruyère, Jarlsberg or sharp cheddar cheese
¼ cup freshly grated Parmesan cheese

Preheat the oven to 350°. In a large skillet, sauté the onion in the oil over medium-low heat until soft and glazed. Add the mushroom and sauté for 1 minute. Remove the skillet from the heat and add the parsley, basil, salt and pepper; mix well and set aside.

In a large bowl, beat the eggs. Add the yogurt or sour cream, prosciutto or ham, shredded cheese and the vegetable mixture and mix well. Pour the egg mixture into an oiled 9-inch square baking pan and sprinkle with the Parmesan cheese. Bake for 25 minutes, or until the eggs are set. Cut into squares and serve warm.

Makes 36 Squares

Appetizers

Sun-Dried Tomato and White Bean Paté

On a first trip to Greece in the sixties, platefuls of tantalizing hummus greeted us at every taverna. Ever since, this spread has been a kitchen staple. In this contemporary version, white beans make an enticing, creamy stand-in for garbanzos. The paté freezes well, so one recipe batch can supply more than one dinner party.

Sun-Dried Tomato Pesto
3 cloves garlic, chopped
1 cup sun-dried, oil-packed or reconstituted if dried tomatoes (see Note)
⅓ cup packed mixed fresh basil and flat-leaf parsley sprigs
2 tablespoons chopped fresh garlic chives or green onion tops
3 tablespoons chopped pistachio nuts or pine nuts
2 tablespoons freshly grated Parmesan cheese
2 tablespoons olive oil

White Bean Paté
2 cans (15 ounces each) cannellini beans, rinsed and drained, or 4 cups cooked Great Northern beans
½ cup lemon juice
4 cloves garlic
3 tablespoons chopped fresh flat-leaf parsley, plus a few sprigs for garnish
2 green onion tops, chopped, or 2 tablespoons chopped fresh chives
½ teaspoon salt
¾ teaspoon ground cumin
Dash freshly ground black pepper
2 tablespoons tahini (see Note)

Sesame crackers or diagonally sliced
celery sticks for accompaniment

To Prepare the Sun-Dried Tomato Pesto: In a food processor workbowl, combine the garlic, tomatoes, herbs and nuts and process until finely minced. Add the cheese and oil and process until well mixed.

To Prepare the White Bean Paté: In a food processor workbowl, combine the beans, lemon juice, garlic, parsley, onion tops or chives, salt, cumin, pepper and tahini and process until almost smooth.

Line three 1-cup plastic containers or custard cups with plastic wrap. Spread ⅓ of the Sun-Dried Tomato Pesto in the bottom of each mold. Top each layer of pesto with a layer of the White Bean Paté, spreading the top smooth. Cover the molds and chill.

Invert the molds onto a serving platter and remove the molds and the plastic wrap. Garnish with a parsley sprig and serve with crackers or celery.

Note: If the tomatoes are dry and brittle, place them in a bowl, add a small amount of hot water, cover with plastic wrap and microwave on high (100%) for 40 to 50 seconds or until plumped. Tahini, sesame paste, can be found in specialty stores or in the international section of the supermarket.

Makes 24 Servings

Sun-Dried Tomato and White Bean Paté

Salads

Caesar Salad in Variation

In the fifties as a young career woman at *Sunset* magazine, I did a multipage spread on Caesar salad and its variations, augmenting the greens with chicken strips, shrimp and grilled steak. Since then, this classic California romaine salad has been popularized in restaurants to become a main dish salad with these additions.

1 clove garlic
6 tablespoons olive oil
1 cup sourdough croutons
1 tablespoon balsamic vinegar
2 tablespoons lemon juice
2 teaspoons Dijon-style mustard
Salt and freshly ground black pepper
    to taste

2 inner heads romaine lettuce
4 anchovy fillets, minced
⅓ cup freshly grated Parmesan cheese
¾ pound cooked small or medium
    shrimp, peeled and deveined,
    or ¾ pound grilled chicken breasts,
    torn or cut into strips

Crush the garlic, place in a small bowl with the oil and let stand for 1 hour or more to allow the garlic to permeate the oil. Remove and discard the garlic.

Preheat the oven to 325°. In a bowl, toss the croutons in 2 tablespoons of the garlic oil. Transfer the croutons to a baking sheet and bake for 10 to 12 minutes, or until lightly toasted.

In a small bowl, whisk together the remaining garlic oil with vinegar, lemon juice and mustard, beating until the mixture is thick and creamy. (For a creamier dressing, whirl the ingredients in a blender.) Season the dressing with salt and pepper.

Tear the romaine into bite-sized pieces and place them in a salad bowl. Add the dressing to taste and toss to coat the greens well with the dressing. Add the anchovies and toss well. Sprinkle with the croutons and cheese. Serve salad portions on plates topped with the shrimp or chicken.

Makes 6 Servings

Western Cobb Salad

This Western-style salad is often layered in a pyramid, but this presentation displays each ingredient like spokes of a wheel. It is reminiscent of the ones I savored at Meier & Frank's Tearoom in Portland, Oregon, in the forties.

About 4 cups butter lettuce pieces
4 hard-cooked eggs
8 strips bacon, cooked until crisp and
    crumbled
1½ cups diced cooked chicken breast
2 medium tomatoes, peeled and diced
1 large avocado, peeled and diced
½ cup crumbled blue or Roquefort
    cheese

Watercress sprigs
⅓ cup canola oil
2 tablespoons white wine vinegar
1 tablespoon fresh lemon juice
1 teaspoon Dijon-style mustard
Salt and freshly ground black pepper
    to taste

Arrange a bed of lettuce on each of the 4 dinner plates. Peel the eggs and rinse them under cold running water; dice the whites and shred the yolks, keeping each separate.

On each plate of greens, arrange one "spoke" each of egg whites, egg yolks, bacon, chicken, tomatoes and avocado. Scatter the cheese over the center and garnish with watercress sprigs.

In a jar, shake together the oil, vinegar, lemon juice, mustard, salt and pepper until blended. Pass the dressing to pour over individual servings.

Note: A handful of alfalfa sprouts is good layered over the greens before topping with the salad ingredients.

Makes 4 Servings

Green Goddess Salad

This famous salad was first created in 1915 at the Palace Hotel in honor of George Arliss, who was appearing in San Francisco that year in William Archer's play, "The Green Goddess." Many times I have enjoyed this salad in Mary Tift's art studio overlooking the Bay in Sausalito. In its simplest form, Green Goddess dressing is ideal on crisp torn romaine. Create a main dish salad by mounding crab, lobster, shrimp or chicken in avocado shells and spooning on the dressing.

⅓ cup mayonnaise
⅓ cup chopped fresh flat-leaf parsley
1½ tablespoons tarragon-flavored
　　white wine vinegar
1 clove garlic, minced
½ teaspoon chopped fresh tarragon,
　　or ⅛ teaspoon dried
2 teaspoons anchovy paste

¼ cup sour cream
Freshly ground black pepper to taste
1 inner head romaine or butter lettuce
2 avocados, halved and pitted
12 ounces crabmeat, small cooked
　　shrimp, lobster meat or diced
　　cooked chicken breast

In a blender container, combine the mayonnaise, parsley, vinegar, garlic, tarragon, anchovy paste, sour cream and pepper. Blend until the parsley is finely minced.

Arrange the romaine on each of 4 salad plates. Top each portion with an avocado half and fill the cavity with seafood or chicken, dividing evenly. Spoon the dressing over the filled avocado and greens.

Makes 4 Servings

Greens, Fruit and Cheese with Shallot Vinaigrette

I find shallots and Dijon-style mustard essential to my basic house dressing. The shallots lend a lively sweet bite and the mustard a good zing. I like to make this dressing in quantity and refrigerate it, ready to use spontaneously for any green salad.

½ cup olive oil
2 tablespoons Dijon-style mustard
3 tablespoons white wine vinegar
¼ cup dry white wine
4 shallots, chopped (about ¼ cup)
1 teaspoon dried tarragon
Dash salt and freshly ground black
   pepper
2 quarts mixed greens: butter
   lettuce, red oak leaf lettuce, arugula
   and/or mache (lamb's lettuce)

2 cups red or green seedless grapes
   or sliced Comice, or 3 Bartlett pears
6 oz. soft mild goat cheese or blue
   cheese
Chopped pistachio nuts, toasted
   hazelnuts or pecans for garnish

In a small jar, shake the oil with the mustard until blended. Add the vinegar, wine, shallots, tarragon, salt and pepper and shake until the ingredients are incorporated. Cover and chill until ready to use. (For a creamier dressing, blend the ingredients with a blender or food processor.)

Place the greens in a salad bowl, add the dressing to taste and toss to coat the greens thoroughly with the dressing. Arrange the greens on each of 12 salad plates. Top the greens with the fruit and cheese, dividing evenly. Sprinkle with the nuts.

Makes 12 Servings

Orange, Lentil and Dried Cherry Salad

Discovering lentils in the fifties came in tandem with my introduction to Greek cuisine. Now I update this versatile salad or light entrée with the sweet-tart tang of dried cherries.

1 cup French green or brown lentils
2½ cups water
¾ teaspoon salt
½ teaspoon dried thyme
2 tablespoons balsamic vinegar
2 tablespoons orange juice
1 tablespoon extra virgin olive oil
2 teaspoons slivered orange zest
½ teaspoon ground allspice
1 teaspoon Dijon-style mustard

⅓ cup finely diced red onion or shallots
⅓ cup dried cherries
2 green onions (white and green parts), chopped
Arugula or small spinach leaves
3 navel oranges, peeled, halved and sliced
3 tablespoons coarsely chopped pistachio nuts or toasted almonds

In a saucepan, combine the lentils, water, salt and thyme and bring to a boil over high heat. Reduce the heat to low, cover and simmer for 25 minutes, or until the lentils are just tender, but still have a slight bite. Drain off any liquid that remains.

In a jar, shake together the vinegar, orange juice, olive oil, orange zest, allspice, mustard and red onion or shallot until the ingredients are incorporated. Stir the vinaigrette into the hot lentils and cool slightly. Cover and chill the lentils until serving time.

Toss the chilled lentils with the cherries and green onions. Arrange a bed of arugula or spinach on each of 4 to 6 serving plates and top with the lentil-cherry mixture, dividing evenly. Ring each plate with the oranges and sprinkle with the nuts.

Makes 4 to 6 Servings

Mushroom, Fennel and Gruyère Salad

In the fifties I discovered the earthy taste-treat of savoring mushrooms raw in a salad. Now in the nineties, anise-flavored fennel replaces the classic celery in this dish, creating an intriguing salad plate. Mince some feathery fronds of the fennel and use as a decorative garnish.

⅓ cup olive oil
3 tablespoons lemon juice
1½ teaspoons Dijon-style mustard
¾ teaspoon grated lemon zest
Salt and freshly ground black pepper
   to taste
2 teaspoons minced fresh tarragon,
   or ½ teaspoon dried
1 pound brown mushrooms,
   thinly sliced

1 bulb fennel, thinly sliced (about
   2 cups)
6 ounces Gruyère or Jarlsberg cheese,
   cut into slivers
4 to 6 cups bite-sized pieces butter
   lettuce or red leaf lettuce
1½ cups red or gold cherry tomatoes,
   halved
¼ cup minced fresh flat-leaf parsley

In a jar, combine the olive oil, lemon juice, mustard, lemon zest, salt, pepper and tarragon and shake until the ingredients are incorporated.

In a bowl, combine the mushrooms, fennel and cheese. Add the dressing to taste and toss to coat the ingredients thoroughly with the dressing. Cover the bowl and chill for 1 hour, tossing once or twice.

Line a platter or serving plates with lettuce. Spoon the mushroom mixture on top of the greens and ring with cherry tomatoes. Garnish with parsley.

Makes 8 Servings

Caramelized Pecan and Apple Salad

This is a recent favorite: sugar-glazed spicy nuts jewel the fruit-and-greens salad. I find it is easy to do a big batch of nuts at one time and refrigerate the surplus for several salads.

Caramelized Pecans
1 tablespoon honey
1 tablespoon sugar
½ teaspoon ground cinnamon
1 tablespoon water
1 cup whole pecans

1 bunch arugula or watercress, stems removed
2 heads butter lettuce, torn into bite-sized pieces

2 large Granny Smith or Fuji apples, or 2 Anjou, red Bartlett or Comice pears, halved, cored and diced
3 tablespoons canola oil
1½ tablespoons red wine vinegar
1 tablespoon balsamic vinegar
2 teaspoons Dijon-style mustard
1 shallot or green onion (white part only), chopped
Salt and freshly ground black pepper to taste

To Prepare the Caramelized Pecans: Preheat the oven to 350°. In a nonstick saucepan, combine the honey, sugar, cinnamon and water and bring to a boil. Add the pecans and simmer for 2 minutes, shaking the pan or stirring frequently to coat the nuts with the sugar mixture. Line a baking sheet with foil and oil the foil lightly or coat it with non-stick spray. Transfer the nuts to the foil and bake for 8 to 10 minutes, or until golden brown, stirring once or twice. Cool the nuts and break apart into small clusters.

In a salad bowl, combine the arugula or watercress, lettuce, and apples or pears.

In a jar, combine the oil, vinegars, mustard, shallot or green onion, salt and pepper and shake until the ingredients are incorporated. Add the dressing to the salad to taste and mix lightly. Place the salad on each of 6 to 8 serving plates and sprinkle with ½ cup of the nuts; reserve the remaining nuts for eating out of hand, or another salad.

Makes 6 to 8 Servings

Salads

Avocado, Pink Grapefruit and Pomegranate Salad

For Thanksgiving celebrations in the sixties, this festive salad reigned. It is an eye-catcher: a pinwheel of pink grapefruit and avocado showered with pomegranate seeds tops greens. To transform it into an entrée salad, omit the seeds and add small cooked shrimp, lobster or crabmeat.

⅓ cup canola oil
2 tablespoons lemon juice
1 tablespoon white wine vinegar
1 teaspoon grated lemon zest
2 teaspoons minced fresh tarragon,
  or ½ teaspoon dried, crumbled
1½ teaspoons Dijon-style mustard

Salt and white pepper to taste
2 pink grapefruits
2 large avocados
Fresh lemon juice
1 head butter lettuce
1 head red leaf lettuce
½ cup pomegranate seeds

In a small jar, combine the canola oil, lemon juice, vinegar, lemon zest, tarragon, mustard, salt and pepper and shake well to incorporate the ingredients.

Peel and section the grapefruits. Peel and slice the avocados and sprinkle the slices with lemon juice to prevent browning. Tear the greens into bite-sized pieces and place in a salad bowl. Add two-thirds of the dressing and toss to coat the greens well.

Place the dressed greens on each of 8 salad plates and arrange the grapefruit sections and avocado slices alternately on top. Sprinkle with the pomegranate seeds and drizzle with the remaining dressing.

Makes 8 Servings

Southwestern Platter Salad

On a trip to Mexico, the street vendors hawking their cups of jicama, cucumber, pineapple and melon sticks inspired this interplay of ingredients. This colorful salad plate has an inviting appeal and stands up well on a buffet table. It is a good mate for barbecued steak, chicken or salmon.

1 inner head romaine lettuce
2 navel oranges, peeled and very
    thinly sliced
1 small cucumber, peeled and thinly
    sliced
1 small sweet red onion, thinly sliced
    and separated into rings
1 cup peeled, thinly sliced jicama
1 small red bell pepper, halved,
    seeded and thinly sliced

¼ cup extra virgin olive oil
¼ cup orange juice
2 tablespoons lemon juice
2 teaspoons grated lemon zest
Salt and freshly ground black pepper
    to taste
2 teaspoons minced fresh oregano,
    or ½ teaspoon dried, crumbled

Tear the romaine into bite-sized pieces and place on a platter. Arrange the oranges, cucumber, onion, jicama and bell pepper decoratively on top of the romaine.

In a jar, combine the oil, orange juice, lemon juice, lemon zest, salt, pepper and oregano and shake until the ingredients are incorporated. Drizzle the dressing over the salad.

Makes 6 to 8 Servings

Spinach Salad with Curry Dressing

Once I discovered the taste-tingling spice blend of curry in the fifties, it anointed my classic spinach salad. This lively dressing is particularly nice with grilled lamb or fish. Use prewashed baby spinach leaves for a fast assembly.

2 tablespoons white wine vinegar
1 tablespoon dry white wine
1 teaspoon soy sauce
½ teaspoon dry mustard
¾ teaspoon curry powder
½ teaspoon sugar
¼ teaspoon freshly ground black pepper
¼ cup canola oil

1 quart baby spinach leaves, or
   1 bunch spinach, stems removed, leaves torn into bite-sized pieces
1 cup halved cherry tomatoes
¼ pound small white or brown mushrooms, sliced
2 tablespoons toasted sunflower kernels or pistachio nuts

In a bowl, combine the vinegar, white wine, soy sauce, dry mustard, curry powder, sugar and pepper and stir until the dry ingredients are dissolved. Whisk in the canola oil and chill until serving time.

In a bowl, combine the spinach, tomatoes and mushrooms. Add the dressing to taste and toss lightly. Sprinkle with the sunflower seeds or pistachio nuts.

Makes 4 Servings

New Potato and Asparagus Salad Caesar

Now that Caesar salad is back in vogue, I remember concocting it with potatoes in the fifties for an article at *Sunset* magazine. Here it gets an uplift with fresh asparagus. Smoked salmon, cut into strips, makes an optional elegant addition.

2 cloves garlic

3 tablespoons extra virgin olive oil

1½ pounds small red potatoes or Yukon gold potatoes, steamed until tender

3 tablespoons dry vermouth or white wine

1 cup ½-inch cubes sweet or sourdough French bread

2 tablespoons balsamic vinegar

1 tablespoon lemon juice

2 teaspoons Dijon-style mustard

2 teaspoons anchovy paste

Salt and freshly ground black pepper to taste

Inner leaves of 1 head romaine lettuce

½ pound asparagus tips, steamed until tender-crisp and chilled

3 tablespoons minced fresh flat-leaf parsley

2 green onions, chopped

¼ cup freshly grated Parmesan cheese

Crush the garlic, place it in a small bowl with the oil and let stand for 30 minutes or more to allow the garlic to permeate the oil. Remove and discard the garlic.

Preheat the oven to 350°. When the potatoes are cool enough to handle, cut them into ¼-inch-thick slices and place them in a bowl. Add the vermouth or wine and toss gently; cool.

In another bowl, toss the bread cubes with 1 tablespoon of the garlic oil. Place the bread cubes on a baking sheet and bake for 10 to 12 minutes, or until golden brown; cool.

Whisk together the remaining garlic oil with the vinegar, lemon juice, mustard, anchovy paste, salt and pepper, beating until the mixture is thick and creamy. Reserve 2 tablespoons of the dressing and pour the remainder over the potatoes; toss gently and chill until serving time.

Arrange spears of romaine on a serving platter and spoon the potatoes and asparagus spears on top. Sprinkle with the parsley, onions and croutons and drizzle with the reserved 2 tablespoons of the dressing. Sprinkle with the cheese.

Makes 6 Servings

Salads

White Bean and Sun-Dried Tomato Salad

Ever since sun-dried tomatoes became popular commercially, I find any excuse to tuck them into a dish. Here they enliven this healthy salad. It is a great choice for a picnic or potluck.

1 pound dried Great Northern or other
   small white beans
½ teaspoon dried thyme
Salt and freshly ground black pepper
   to taste
4 cloves garlic, minced
⅓ cup lemon juice
3 tablespoons white wine vinegar
¼ cup olive oil
1 tablespoon Dijon-style mustard

1 tablespoon minced lemon zest
1 medium-sized red onion,
   finely chopped
1 cup slivered dry sun-dried tomatoes
½ cup minced fresh flat-leaf parsley
Salad greens
1 cup red cherry tomatoes, halved
1 cup gold cherry tomatoes, halved
4 cooked chicken breast halves,
   cut into ½-inch strips (optional)

Place the beans in a large pot, cover with water by at least 2 inches and soak for at least 8 hours, covered, in the refrigerator.

Drain the beans and cover with fresh water by at least 2 inches. Add the thyme and bring to a boil over high heat. Reduce the heat to low, cover and simmer for 1 hour, or until the beans are tender; add the salt and pepper about halfway through the cooking time. Drain the beans and stir in the garlic. In a bowl, mix together the lemon juice, vinegar, oil, mustard, lemon zest and onion. Add the mixture to the beans, toss well and chill.

In a small saucepan, cover the sun-dried tomatoes with about ½ cup water and simmer for 1 minute; remove from the heat and cool.

At serving time, toss the bean mixture with the plumped dried tomatoes and parsley. Transfer the salad to a serving bowl, tuck in the greens around the edge of the bowl and garnish with the cherry tomatoes. Arrange the chicken strips, if using, on serving plates with the salad.

Makes 10 to 12 Servings

Salads

Tabbouleh

Looking back, this was my first discovery of how captivating a "foreign dish" could be when I tasted it at a high school potluck. Since then I have embellished the salad in this fashion. This is a versatile tabbouleh; if desired, add 2 tablespoons chopped lemon grass, preserved lemon or minced fresh basil for variation.

1 cup cracked wheat or bulgur wheat
⅔ cup water
¼ cup lemon juice
¼ cup extra virgin olive oil
¾ teaspoon salt
¼ teaspoon freshly ground black
   pepper
1 teaspoon ground allspice
1 cup minced fresh flat-leaf parsley
1 bunch green onions, chopped

2 cloves garlic, minced (optional)
3 tablespoons chopped pistachio nuts
Assorted greens: butter lettuce,
   red oak leaf lettuce or radicchio
Romaine lettuce spears (optional)
½ pound small cooked shrimp or
   crabmeat (optional)
1 cup seedless red or green grapes
   (optional)

Place the cracked wheat or bulgur in a sieve and rinse under cold running water; drain and place in a bowl. Add the water and let the wheat stand until puffed and softened, about 30 minutes.

In a small bowl, mix the lemon juice, oil, salt, pepper and allspice and add to the bowl with the wheat, mixing lightly with a fork to separate the grains. Stir in the parsley, onions and garlic, if using, and chill until serving time. Stir in the nuts.

Line a conical mold or bowl with plastic wrap and pack in the salad; unmold the salad onto a platter lined with the greens. Ring the platter with small romaine spears for scooping, or with seafood and grapes, if desired.

Makes 6 Servings

Les Halles Onion Soup

The original bustling Parisian food market—Les Halles—served bowls of this cheese-crusted onion soup, the majority in the predawn hours to a colorful mingling of society and workers. The soup became a classic around the world. The stock can be made in advance and frozen; or for speed on short notice, use concentrated beef stock base.

Rich Beef Stock
2 pounds beef and veal shank bones
2 quarts water
1 carrot, diced
1 onion, roughly chopped
1½ teaspoons salt
1 bay leaf
2 cloves garlic, minced

1 tablespoon olive oil
5 large yellow onions, sliced
Salt and freshly ground black pepper
  to taste
6 ½-inch-thick slices buttered, toasted
  French bread
½ cup shredded Gruyère cheese
¼ cup freshly grated Parmesan cheese

To Prepare the Rich Beef Stock: Preheat the oven to 425°. Place the beef and veal bones in an open roasting pan and roast for 30 minutes, or until browned. Transfer the roasted bones to a stockpot and add the water, carrot, onion, salt, bay leaf and garlic and bring just to a boil over high heat. Quickly reduce the heat to low and simmer for 2 hours. Strain the stock, discarding the solids, and cool to room temperature over an ice bath, stirring frequently to help cooling. Refrigerate the stock until chilled, preferably overnight, and lift off and discard the solidified fat that sits on the top of the stock.

In a large stockpot, heat the oil over low heat. Add the onions and slowly sauté them until golden brown, stirring occasionally. Add the Rich Beef Stock and simmer for 30 minutes. Season with salt and pepper.

Preheat the broiler. Ladle the soup into 6 ovenproof soup bowls. Float a slice of toasted bread on the surface of each bowl of soup and sprinkle with the mixed cheeses. Place the soup bowls under the broiler until the cheese melts and lightly browns.

Makes 6 Servings

Soups

Ginger Carrot Soup

In the seventies as I stripped away surplus fat in recipes and wrote *Gourmet Cooking the Slim Way*, this became a reliable spur-of-the-moment soup as the ingredients were generally on hand. Ginger lends a teasing flair.

3 cups water
1 large onion, chopped
6 large carrots, cut into 1-inch chunks
⅛ teaspoon nutmeg or mace
1 tablespoon minced fresh ginger
2 cloves garlic, minced
Dash hot pepper sauce
2 tablespoons peanut butter,
   or ¼ cup peanuts

Salt and freshly ground black pepper
   to taste
¼ cup plain yogurt or dry white wine
   (optional)
Chopped peanuts or pistachio nuts
   for garnish
Chopped fresh chives or diced red-
   skinned apple for garnish

In a saucepan, combine the water, onion, carrots, nutmeg or mace, ginger, garlic and hot pepper sauce. Bring the mixture to a boil over high heat. Reduce the heat to low, cover the pan and simmer until the vegetables are very tender, about 20 minutes.

Cool the mixture slightly and puree with a blender or a food processor with the peanut butter or peanuts. Return the soup to the pan and season with salt and pepper. Stir in the yogurt or wine, if desired, and heat through. Ladle the hot soup into bowls and garnish with nuts and chives or apple.

Makes 6 Servings

Soups

Sherried Mushroom Soup

Since the blender first arrived in my kitchen in the fifties, this has been a favorite winter treat. Originally whipping cream enriched it. In the seventies I stripped the cream away after discovering yogurt gives ample body and a nice tang.

1 tablespoon olive oil
¾ pound small brown or white
   mushrooms, chopped
1 medium onion, finely chopped
2 tablespoons chopped celery leaves
3 cups chicken broth
2 cloves garlic, minced

Salt and freshly ground black pepper
   to taste
1 teaspoon chopped fresh tarragon, or
   ¼ teaspoon dried
2 cups milk
¼ cup dry sherry
Plain yogurt or sour cream for garnish

In a saucepan, heat the oil over medium-high heat. Add the mushrooms and onion and sauté until glazed. Add the celery leaves, broth and garlic and bring to a boil over high heat. Reduce the heat to low, cover the pan and simmer for 10 minutes.

Cool the soup slightly and puree with a blender or food processor. Return to the pureed soup to the pan. Add the salt, pepper, tarragon and milk and heat through. Stir in the sherry.

Serve the soup in bowls garnished with yogurt or sour cream.

Makes 6 Servings

Vegetable Soup with Pesto

I've savored many variations of this great soup on trips to the Provence region of France and Italy. It is especially good with a big bowl of homemade pesto to embellish it.

1 quart chicken broth
1 large red potato, diced
1 carrot, thinly sliced
1 medium zucchini, thinly sliced
1 yellow crookneck squash,
   thinly sliced
1 small leek (white part only), sliced
⅓ cup shelled fresh peas

1 tomato, peeled and chopped
2 tablespoons minced fresh flat-leaf
   parsley
Salt and freshly ground black pepper
   to taste
Basil Pesto, page 51, or use purchased
¼ cup freshly grated Parmesan cheese

In a large saucepan, bring the broth to a boil over high heat. Add the potato and carrot, reduce the heat to low, cover the pan and simmer for 10 minutes. Add the zucchini, crookneck squash and leek and simmer for 8 to 10 minutes, or until the vegetables are tender-crisp. Add the peas, tomato and parsley and simmer for 2 minutes. Season with salt and pepper. Ladle the soup into bowls and pass the Basil Pesto and the cheese.

Makes 4 Servings

The Farmer's Soup

I have been making this hearty soup since my early trips to France in the sixties. Sometimes red Bliss potatoes replace russets; then, I leave their pink skins intact. The cheese and parsley flourish on top gives a teasing finish.

3 medium leeks
2 tablespoons olive oil
1 large yellow onion, chopped
1½ quarts chicken broth
3 large russet potatoes, peeled and diced
2 teaspoons chopped fresh tarragon, or ½ teaspoon dried

Salt and freshly ground black pepper to taste
3 tablespoons minced fresh flat-leaf parsley
1 cup shredded Gruyère, Jarlsberg or Emmentaler cheese

Trim the leeks and cut them in half lengthwise. Wash the leeks well under cold running water to remove any sand. Finely chop the leeks.

In a large saucepan, heat the oil over medium heat and sauté the onion until soft, about 2 minutes. Add the broth and potatoes, cover and simmer for 15 minutes.

Add the leeks, tarragon, salt and pepper and simmer for 10 minutes longer, or until the vegetables are soft. Coarsely mash the vegetables with a potato masher. Ladle the soup into bowls and sprinkle with the parsley and cheese.

Makes 6 to 8 Servings

Black Bean Soup

For many years the whole family enjoyed going for Christmas soup at the home of my eldest's first grade teacher, Pat Robinson. This was often one of three soups, bubbling in the kitchen ready for ladling into hand-thrown pottery bowls. She would invite friends and neighbors, serving more than 150 guests a season.

1 pound dried black beans
1 small ham shank, about 1 pound
2 medium onions, chopped
1 stalk celery with leaves,
   or 1 bulb fennel, chopped
2 carrots, chopped
3 cloves garlic, minced
1 bay leaf

½ teaspoon dried oregano
½ teaspoon ground allspice
1 small dried red chile, seeds removed
3 tablespoons red wine vinegar
1 can (8 ounces) tomato sauce
Salt and freshly ground black pepper
   to taste

Accompaniments: Plain yogurt or sour cream, lime wedges, chopped fresh cilantro and chopped fresh chives or green onion tops

Place the beans in a large pot, cover with water by at least 2 inches and let soak for at least 8 hours, covered, in the refrigerator.

Drain the beans, add fresh water to the pot with the ham shank, onions, celery or fennel, carrots, garlic, bay leaf, oregano, allspice and chile and bring to a boil over high heat. Reduce the heat to low, cover and simmer for 1 to 1¼ hours, or until the beans are almost tender. Add the vinegar and tomato sauce and simmer until the beans are tender, about 20 to 30 minutes longer. Discard the bay leaf. Remove the ham shank from the soup. Chop the ham meat into small pieces, discarding the bone.

Transfer about ¼ of the beans and some cooking liquid to a blender container or food processor workbowl and process until smooth. Return the bean puree to the soup pot with the chopped ham.

Heat the soup through and season with salt and pepper. (If desired, you can cool the soup at this point and refrigerate until serving time. Heat the soup through to serve.) To serve, ladle the soup into bowls and pass bowls of the accompaniments.

Makes 8 to 10 Servings

Ranchero Soup in a Pumpkin Tureen

This colorful soup from the Gold Rush days is a great way to greet Halloween. Accompany with crispy tortilla chips and a sliced orange and jicama salad for a full meal.

1 teaspoon olive oil
1 onion, chopped
6 chicken legs or thighs (about
   1¼ pounds), skinned
1 quart water
2 to 3 celery leaves, chopped
2 cloves garlic, minced
Salt and freshly ground black pepper
   to taste
½ teaspoon ground cumin
½ teaspoon dried oregano
Small piece hot red chile (optional)
2 small zucchini, sliced

1½ cups diced steamed butternut
   squash or banana squash
2 small yellow crookneck squash,
   sliced
2 ears corn, husked and cut into 1-inch
   slices, or kernels cut from the cob
1 pumpkin, about 3-pounds
¼ cup chopped fresh cilantro
3 tablespoons roasted sunflower seeds
1 small avocado, peeled and diced
1 small red bell pepper, seeded and
   diced (optional)

In a large saucepan, heat the oil over medium heat. Add the onion and sauté until soft. Add the chicken, water, celery leaves, garlic, salt, pepper, cumin, oregano and hot chile, if desired, and bring to a boil over high heat. Reduce the heat to low, cover the pan and simmer for 30 to 40 minutes, or until the chicken is tender. Lift the chicken from the broth. Remove the chicken meat from the bones and tear into strips; discard the bones. Skim the fat from the top of the broth. Bring the broth back to a simmer, add the squash and corn and simmer for 2 minutes. Add the chicken meat and heat through.

While the soup is simmering, preheat the oven to 375°. Cut off the top of the pumpkin and scoop out the seeds. Place the pumpkin on an ovenproof platter and bake for 15 minutes, or until heated through.

Pour the hot soup into the pumpkin shell. At serving time, ladle the soup from the pumpkin shell into bowls and sprinkle with the cilantro and sunflower seeds. Garnish with the avocado and red pepper, if desired.

Makes 6 Servings

Gazpacho Monterey

One of my early food styling assignments involved this photogenic soup, pictured with a dazzling array of condiments alongside. I have always called this Monterey style— not knowing why.

1 medium cucumber, peeled and finely chopped
1 small red onion, finely chopped
5 large vine-ripened tomatoes, peeled and finely chopped
2 cloves garlic, minced
1 cup beef broth
1 cup vegetable juice cocktail

2 tablespoons fresh lime juice
2 tablespoons olive oil
Salt and freshly ground black pepper to taste
1 tablespoon chopped fresh basil, or ¾ teaspoon dried
6 ice cubes

Accompaniments: Diced avocado, sunflower seeds and/or chopped pistachio nuts

In a medium bowl, combine the cucumber, onion, tomatoes, garlic, broth, vegetable juice, lime juice, oil, salt, pepper and basil and mix well. Cover the bowl and refrigerate until completely chilled.

Ladle the chilled soup into cold soup bowls. Add an ice cube to each bowl and pass bowls of the accompaniments.

Makes 6 Servings

Cioppino

In the fifties when a meaty 3-pound Dungeness crab cost less than a dollar, we savored this fish stew with San Francisco sourdough French bread, sweet butter and a bottle of Wente grey Riesling. When serving, offer oversized napkins or steaming hot towels for cleaning hands, and bowls to discard the shells.

2 tablespoons olive oil
1 carrot, diced
4 green onions, chopped
1 can (15 ounces) tomato puree
1 bottle (8 ounces) clam juice
½ cup dry white wine
1 teaspoon minced fresh basil, or ¼ teaspoon dried
1 teaspoon minced fresh thyme, or ¼ teaspoon dried

1 teaspoon minced fresh oregano, or ¼ teaspoon dried
1 live Dungeness crab, about 3 pounds (see *Note*)
12 clams in the shell
1 pound red snapper fillet, cut into 1-inch chunks
2 tablespoons minced fresh flat-leaf parsley

In a large saucepan, heat the oil over medium-high heat. Add the carrot and onions and sauté until the vegetables are limp. Add the tomato puree, clam juice, wine, basil, thyme and oregano. Cover the pan and simmer for 30 minutes.

Clean and crack the crab and add it to the soup with the clams and fish fillet. Simmer for 10 to 15 minutes, until the clams open and the crab and fish are cooked through. Serve the cioppino in large bowls and garnish with parsley.

Note: To clean and crack a Dungeness crab: First kill the crab by placing it upside down on a cutting board and hold a sharp heavy knife or cleaver so the blade rests sharp side down in the center of the crab's underside. Hit the knife or cleaver with a sharp blow with a hammer. Wash the crab well under cold running water. Twist claws and legs off; then pry and pull off the top shell. Remove and discard the gray gills and spongy parts. Save the cream crab "butter" for a spread, if you like. Crack the body section, claws and legs with a hammer.

Makes 4 Servings

Fisherman's Stew

This flavor-packed full-meal soup is surprisingly easy to assemble. It was a discovery on a press trip to the picturesque seaport of Honfleur, France. You can use halibut or another firm white fish in place of the snapper.

1 tablespoon olive oil
1 medium onion, chopped
1 medium to large leek, (white part only) chopped
3 stalks fennel, chopped (about 1 cup)
4 cups fish or chicken broth
¾ cup dry white wine or vermouth
3 medium Yukon gold or white potatoes, peeled and cut into 1-inch chunks

1 bay leaf
½ teaspoon fennel seeds
1 pound red snapper fillets
Salt and freshly ground black pepper to taste
Minced fresh dill, fennel or flat-leaf parsley for garnish

In a large saucepan, heat the oil over medium heat. Add the onion, leek and fennel and sauté until soft. Add the stock and wine or vermouth and bring to a boil over high heat. Add the potatoes, bay leaf and fennel seeds and return to the boil. Reduce the heat to low, cover and simmer until the vegetables are tender, about 20 minutes.

Cut the fish into small chunks and add them to the soup. Cover the pan and simmer for about 8 to 10 minutes, or until the fish is cooked through. Remove the bay leaf and discard. Season with salt and pepper and serve garnished with the herbs.

Makes 6 Servings

Soups

Lentil Soup with Sausage

My Greek mother-in-law, Yaya, indulged us with this wholesome soup. A variety of sausages can flavor it; it is excellent without sausages as well.

2 cups small French green or
  brown lentils
1 medium onion, chopped
1 stalk celery with leaves, chopped
1 carrot, chopped
8 sun-dried tomatoes, slivered
2 quarts chicken broth, beef broth
  or water
2 cloves garlic, minced

½ teaspoon dried thyme
1 bay leaf
¼ cup red wine vinegar or dry red
  wine
3 tablespoons tomato paste
2 Polish sausages, summer sausages
  or Italian sausages
Salt and freshly ground black pepper
  to taste

In a saucepan, combine the lentils, onion, celery, carrot, tomatoes, broth or water, garlic, thyme and bay leaf and bring to a boil. Reduce the heat to low, cover the pan and simmer for 30 minutes, or until the lentils are almost tender.

Discard the bay leaf. Add the vinegar, tomato paste and sausages and simmer until the sausages are cooked through, about 15 minutes.

Remove the sausages from the soup. Cut the sausages into bite-sized pieces and return them to the pan. Season the soup with salt and pepper, heat through and serve.

Makes 8 to 10 Servings

Spicy Lamb Meatball Soup

This aromatic full-meal soup is a takeoff on a Moroccan recipe. It has been part of my repertoire since the seventies. At times, ground turkey has replaced the lamb.

1 tablespoon olive oil
1 large onion, chopped
1 tablespoon minced fresh ginger
2 cloves garlic, minced
1 teaspoon ground cumin
½ teaspoon ground allspice
Freshly ground black pepper to taste
3 medium carrots, sliced
1 stalk celery or fennel, chopped
1 large sweet potato, peeled and diced
6 cups low-fat chicken broth
3 tablespoons tomato paste

Lamb Meatballs

12 ounces lean ground lamb
1 egg white
3 tablespoons minced fresh cilantro or
  flat-leaf parsley
2 cloves garlic, minced
1 green onion, finely chopped
Salt and freshly ground black pepper
  to taste

⅓ cup minced fresh cilantro or
  flat-leaf parsley for garnish

In a large saucepan, heat the oil over medium heat. Add the onion and sauté for 2 minutes. Add the ginger, garlic, cumin, allspice, pepper, carrots, celery or fennel and sweet potato and sauté for 2 minutes. Add the chicken broth and tomato paste and bring to a boil over high heat. Reduce the heat to low, cover the pan and simmer for 10 minutes.

To Prepare the Lamb Meatballs: In a bowl, mix together the ground lamb, egg white, cilantro or parsley, garlic, green onion, salt and pepper. Shape the mixture into ¾-inch balls.

Drop the meatballs into the simmering soup and cook for 5 to 7 minutes, or until the meatballs are cooked through.

Preferably, cook the soup to this point and chill for several hours or overnight. When cold, skim off any fat that sits on the surface. Heat the soup through, ladle into bowls and garnish with cilantro or parsley.

Makes 6 Servings

Soups

Pasta & Grains

Pasta with Pesto

This classic Italian dish is superb for a simple dinner, accompanied by crusty country bread and a starter of melon wrapped with prosciutto. Finish off with gelato, preferably home-churned, or zabaglione.

Basil Pesto
2 cups packed fresh basil leaves
3 tablespoons pine nuts or coarsely chopped pistachio nuts
2 large cloves garlic

⅓ cup olive oil
3 tablespoons freshly grated Parmesan cheese, plus more for passing

8 ounces fresh or dried fettuccine

To Prepare the Basil Pesto: In a food processor workbowl, combine the basil, pine nuts or pistachios and garlic and process until finely minced. Add the oil and cheese and process until mixed. (If making ahead, transfer the pesto to a small bowl, cover and chill until needed.)

In a large pot of boiling salted water, cook the pasta until just tender to the bite, *al dente*, about 3 minutes for fresh pasta or 11 minutes for dried pasta. Reserve 2 to 3 tablespoons of the pasta cooking liquid and drain the pasta. Transfer the pasta to a warm serving bowl and keep warm.

Mix the reserved pasta liquid with the pesto. Add the pesto to the pasta and mix until well coated. Serve immediately on warm plates. Pass the cheese.

Makes 4 Servings

Pasta & Grains

Pasta Primavera

At the start of the pasta craze in America, this dish was one of the first featured in my cooking classes. It is smart to alternate the vegetables to suit the season, introducing asparagus, leeks and red onions in the spring, or broccoli in mid-winter, for the pea pods and squash.

12 snow pea pods, trimmed
1 medium zucchini, cut into slivers
1 yellow crookneck squash, cut into
  slivers
½ pound dried fettuccine or tagliarini
2 tablespoons olive oil
1 tablespoon pine nuts or coarsely
  chopped pistachio nuts

2 tablespoons Basil Pesto, page 51,
  or use purchased
¼ cup heavy cream
8 cherry tomatoes, halved
3 tablespoons freshly grated Parmesan
  or Romano cheese

Separately cook the pea pods, zucchini and crookneck squash in boiling water for about 1 minute, or until tender-crisp; cool under cold running water and drain well.

In a large pot of boiling salted water, cook the pasta until just tender to the bite, *al dente*, about 10 minutes; drain. Transfer the pasta to a warm serving bowl and keep warm.

In a large skillet, heat the oil over medium heat and add the partially cooked vegetables, nuts, Basil Pesto and cream. Cook, stirring, for 1 to 2 minutes, or until the sauce reduces slightly. Add tomatoes and heat through. Pour the vegetable mixture over the pasta and mix lightly. Sprinkle with the cheese and serve immediately.

Makes 4 Servings

Linguine with Vegetables and Provolone

Ever since a first trip to Italy in the sixties when I dined at Alfredo's in Rome, I have enjoyed concocting pasta entrées. It wasn't until much later that pasta became a culinary rage in the States. Here smoky-flavored cheese melts to cloak hot pasta and garden vegetables.

½ pound dried linguine
2 tablespoons olive oil
1 clove garlic, minced
2 green onions, chopped
2 small zucchini, sliced
¼ pound small white mushrooms, sliced

1 medium tomato, chopped
Salt and freshly ground black pepper to taste
3 tablespoons minced fresh basil
2 tablespoons minced fresh flat-leaf parsley
1 cup shredded provolone cheese

In a large pot of boiling salted water, cook the linguine until just tender to the bite, *al dente*, about 10 to 12 minutes; drain. Transfer the pasta to a serving bowl and keep warm.

In a large skillet, heat the oil over medium-high heat. Add the garlic, green onions, zucchini and mushrooms and sauté until glazed. Add the tomato, salt and pepper, cover the skillet and simmer for 2 to 3 minutes, or until the zucchini is tender-crisp.

Transfer the vegetable mixture to the bowl with the pasta. Add the basil, parsley and cheese and mix gently until the cheese melts.

Makes 4 Servings

Spaghetti with Browned Butter and Meat Sauce

This was a family favorite of my Greek mother-in-law and a recipe I made in quantity for family meals. It is excellent in casserole pasta dishes, rolled up in tortillas with beans or stuffed in pita pockets along with chopped green onions, tomatoes and feta cheese. Sometimes I have substituted ground turkey or lean ground pork for the beef.

1 tablespoon olive oil
2 large onions, chopped
2 pounds lean ground beef
1 teaspoon whole mixed pickling spice,
   tied in a cheesecloth bag
3 cloves garlic, minced
2 cans (6 ounces each) tomato paste
Salt and freshly ground black pepper
   to taste

2 tablespoons red wine vinegar
2 cups water, plus more if necessary
8 ounces dried spaghetti
2 tablespoons butter
⅓ cup freshly grated Parmesan or
   Romano cheese

In a large skillet, heat the oil over medium heat. Add the onions and sauté until soft; transfer the onions to a plate. Add the beef to the skillet and sauté until browned and crumbly. Return the onions to the pan. Add the pickling spice to the pan with the garlic, tomato paste, salt, pepper, vinegar and water. Cover the pan and simmer the sauce, stirring occasionally, for 3 hours, or until the sauce is thickened, adding more water if necessary. Cool the sauce. (Ladle the extra cooled sauce into freezer containers and freeze until needed).

In a large pot of boiling salted water, cook the spaghetti until just tender to the bite, *al dente*, about 10 minutes; drain and transfer to a bowl. If necessary, heat the meat sauce in a saucepan until heated through.

In a skillet, heat the butter over medium heat until bubbly and slightly browned and pour over the spaghetti; mix lightly. Spoon the spaghetti onto serving plates, top with the meat sauce and sprinkle with the cheese.

Makes 4 Servings

Lasagna

This party dish is smart to assemble in advance, chill and bake later. It was a favorite in the sixties, paired with Caesar salad, sourdough bread and lemon cheese tart.

1 tablespoon olive oil
1 onion, chopped
1 carrot, grated
1 stalk celery, chopped
1 pound lean ground beef
½ pound mild or hot Italian bulk
   sausage
1 teaspoon dried basil
1 can (15 ounces) tomato puree
3 tablespoons tomato paste

3 cloves garlic, minced
Salt and freshly ground black pepper
   to taste
¼ cup dry red wine
12 ounces dried lasagna noodles
1 pound ricotta cheese
12 ounces mozzarella cheese, grated
½ cup freshly grated Romano or
   Parmesan cheese

In a large skillet, heat the oil over medium heat. Add the onion, carrot and celery and sauté until softened. Add the beef and sausage and cook until browned and crumbly. Add the basil, tomato puree, tomato paste, garlic, salt, pepper and wine and mix well. Cover the saucepan and simmer for 1½ hours.

Preheat the oven to 350°. In a large pot of boiling salted water, cook the noodles until just tender to the bite, *al dente*, about 10 to 12 minutes. Drain the noodles, rinse under cold water and drain again.

Arrange about one-third of the noodles in a greased 9-x-13-inch baking pan. Spread one-third of the meat sauce over the noodles and top with one-third each of the ricotta and mozzarella. Repeat the layering process two more times. Sprinkle the top of the casserole with the Romano or Parmesan cheese and bake uncovered for 30 to 40 minutes, or until browned.

Makes 12 Servings

Pasta & Grains

Macaroni and Meat Squares

Greek holiday occasions often incorporated this macaroni and cheese dish, called Pastitsio, in the menu. It is great for a buffet gathering, as it cuts neatly into squares for serving and can be made a day in advance. Serve it hot or at room temperature.

1 tablespoon olive oil
2 large onions, finely chopped
2½ pounds lean ground beef
2 cans (8 ounces each) tomato sauce
Salt and freshly ground black pepper
   to taste
3 cloves garlic, minced
½ teaspoon dried oregano
1 stick cinnamon
¼ cup butter

¼ cup flour
3 cups milk
½ teaspoon salt
Freshly ground black pepper to taste
Freshly ground nutmeg to taste
6 eggs
16 ounces dried elbow macaroni
1½ cups grated Romano cheese
Cinnamon for dusting

In a large skillet, heat the oil over medium heat. Add the onions and sauté until golden. Add the beef and cook until browned and crumbly. Add the tomato sauce, salt, pepper, garlic, oregano and cinnamon stick. Cover the pan and simmer the sauce for 30 minutes, or until thickened. Remove the cinnamon stick.

In a saucepan, melt the butter over medium-low heat and blend in the flour. Gradually stir in the milk and cook, stirring, until thickened. Season with salt, pepper and nutmeg. In a bowl, beat the eggs until light and stir the hot sauce into the eggs until well blended.

Preheat the oven to 350°. In a large pot of boiling salted water, cook the macaroni until just tender to the bite, *al dente*, about 12 minutes. Drain the macaroni, rinse under cold water and drain again.

In a greased 9-by-13-inch baking pan, alternate layers of macaroni, meat sauce, and ¾ cup of the cheese. Dust the top lightly with cinnamon. Pour the custard sauce over the casserole and sprinkle with the remaining ¾ cup of the cheese. Bake for 45 minutes, or until the custard sauce is set. Cool slightly and cut into squares.

Makes 12 Servings

Pasta & Grains

Tomato and Portobello Polenta Pie

Polenta was a popular Italian dish when I arrived in California and I learned to prepare it in many styles. This is a recent version, accented with the wonderful meaty portobello mushrooms and Roma tomatoes. This dish makes a delicious accompaniment to grilled chicken, fish or pork. Or, enjoy it as a vegetarian-style entrée.

1 cup polenta
2 cups cold water
1 can (14 ounces) chicken broth
Salt and freshly ground black pepper
   to taste
2 tablespoons olive oil
1 tablespoon balsamic vinegar
2 cloves garlic, minced

1 large portobello mushroom cap,
   thinly sliced and cut into 1-inch
   lengths, or ½ pound white or
   brown mushrooms, sliced
2 Roma tomatoes, chopped
½ cup shredded Gruyère cheese
¼ cup mixed minced fresh chives,
   flat-leaf parsley and tarragon

In a bowl, soak the polenta in the cold water for 10 minutes.

In a large saucepan, bring the broth to a boil and stir in the soaked polenta and any remaining water. Bring the mixture back to a boil, reduce the heat to low and simmer, stirring occasionally, for 15 minutes. Stir in the salt, pepper and 1 tablespoon of the oil. Transfer the polenta mixture to a greased 9-inch pie pan.

Preheat the broiler. In a medium bowl, stir together the vinegar, remaining 1 tablespoon of the oil and the garlic. Add the mushrooms, toss to coat with the vinegar mixture and transfer to a foil-lined baking pan. Broil the mushrooms for 2 minutes, turning once. Spoon the broiled mushrooms over the polenta and top with the tomatoes and cheese. Broil until the cheese is browned. Sprinkle with the herbs and cut into wedges to serve.

Makes 6 Servings

Cassoulet

This old-fashioned French bean stew is a traditional dish from the Languedoc region of France, popular in local bistros. It is wonderful for an informal party dinner on a wintry night. It is also great to tote to a ski cabin for a weekend sojourn.

1½ cups dried Great Northern beans, soaked for 8 hours or overnight
3 slices bacon, diced
2 medium onions, chopped
1½ pounds boneless pork, cut into 1-inch cubes
2 cups dry red wine
1 cup beef broth

3 tablespoons brandy or cognac
4 cloves garlic, minced
2 tablespoons tomato paste
Salt and freshly ground black pepper to taste
½ teaspoon crumbled dried thyme
1 pound mild Italian garlic sausages
Minced fresh flat-leaf parsley for garnish

Place the beans in a large pot, cover with water by at least 2 inches and let soak for at least 8 hours, covered, in the refrigerator.

Preheat the oven to 350°. In a large saucepan, sauté the bacon and onions until glazed; push the bacon and onions to the sides of the saucepan and drain off the extra fat. Add the pork to the saucepan and cook until browned on all sides. Add the wine, broth, brandy or cognac, garlic, tomato paste, salt, pepper, and thyme and bring to a boil. Transfer the mixture to a large greased casserole and stir in the beans. Cover the casserole and bake for 2 hours.

In a saucepan, cover the sausages with water and bring to a boil; cover the pan, remove from the heat and set aside for 20 minutes. Drain the sausages and slice them on the diagonal. Arrange the sausage slices on top of the casserole and continue baking for 20 minutes, or until the beans are tender. Sprinkle with parsley and serve hot.

Makes 8 to 10 Servings

Orzo with Sun-Dried Tomatoes and Feta

My introduction to orzo, tear-shaped pasta, first came as an accompaniment to my Mother-in-law, Yaya's succulent roast leg of lamb and baby artichoke hearts. As cold pasta became stylish in the nineties, I tried it this way. I have even made this recipe in a ten-pound batch for a large-scale picnic—it is always a winner. Crusty country bread or focaccia and pesto make tasty accompaniments.

8 ounces dried orzo
¼ cup olive oil
1½ tablespoons lemon juice
1 shallot or green onion (white part only), finely chopped
1 tablespoon minced fresh dill or basil, or ¾ teaspoon dried
2 teaspoons minced fresh oregano, or ½ teaspoon dried

Salt and freshly ground black pepper to taste
¼ cup minced fresh flat-leaf parsley
½ cup slivered sun-dried tomatoes, oil-packed or reconstituted if dried
¾ cup crumbled feta cheese
⅓ cup toasted pine nuts or coarsely chopped pistachio nuts
Arugula or oak leaf lettuce

In a large pot of boiling salted water, cook the orzo until just tender to the bite, *al dente*, about 12 minutes; drain, letting some liquid cling to the pasta. Cool the orzo for a few minutes and transfer it to a serving bowl.

In another bowl, stir together the oil, lemon juice, shallot or green onion, dill or basil, oregano, salt and pepper. Add the oil mixture to the bowl with the pasta and toss to coat well. Stir in the parsley, tomatoes and feta cheese and chill until serving time.

When ready to serve, sprinkle the pasta with the nuts and tuck the arugula or lettuce decoratively around the edge of the bowl.

Makes 4 to 6 Servings

Pasta & Grains

Spicy Ginger Couscous

Couscous cooks in minutes, making it a staple in my household over the years. For an attractive presentation, line small custard cups or soufflé dishes with plastic wrap, spoon in the hot couscous, pat down and invert onto dinner plates. Or for a buffet, pack the couscous in one round-bottomed bowl, first lined with plastic wrap, and turn it out onto a platter.

1 teaspoon olive oil
1 small sweet onion, chopped
2 teaspoons minced fresh ginger
½ teaspoon ground allspice
½ teaspoon cinnamon
8 threads saffron

1 ⅓ cups chicken broth
⅔ cup couscous
¼ cup golden raisins or dried currants
2 tablespoons chopped pistachio nuts
  or slivered almonds

In a skillet, heat the oil over medium heat. Add the onion, ginger, allspice, cinnamon and saffron and sauté until the onion is soft and glazed.

Add the broth to the skillet and bring to a boil. Stir in the couscous and raisins or currants. Cover the skillet, remove from the heat and let stand for 10 minutes.

Sprinkle with the nuts and serve hot.

Makes 4 Servings

Asian Sesame Noodle Salad

Admittedly, this dish is a recent newcomer, but it's so good it has become a standby the past year at Kappa Kappa Gamma alumnae salad potlucks. It is a superb dish to have handy in the refrigerator for a summer luncheon or supper. The pasta can be varied, from thin spaghetti to udon noodles. The fruit garnish refreshes all. Other fruits in season, such as sliced nectarines, apricots or plums, can replace the melon and grapes.

3 tablespoons low-sodium soy sauce
3 tablespoons Asian sesame oil
3 tablespoons creamy or chunky
   peanut butter
2 tablespoons rice vinegar
1 tablespoon dark brown sugar
2 cloves garlic, minced
2 teaspoons minced fresh ginger

8 ounces dried thin spaghetti or
   udon noodles
Salt and cayenne pepper to taste
3 green onions (white and green
   parts), chopped
½ cantaloupe, cut into crescents
½ cup seedless green or red grapes
¼ cup minced fresh cilantro

In a large bowl, whisk together the soy sauce, sesame oil, peanut butter, vinegar, brown sugar, garlic and ginger; set aside.

In a large pot of boiling salted water, cook the pasta according to the package directions, until just tender to the bite, *al dente*. Drain the pasta and place it in a bowl; cool to room tempature. Add the sesame mixture and toss well. Add the salt, cayenne and onions and mix well. Cover and refrigerate for at least 1 hour, until serving time.

To serve, arrange the salad on a serving platter, ring with cantaloupe and grapes and sprinkle with cilantro.

Makes 4 Servings

Pasta & Grains

Tortilla Pizzas

In the seventies as I was stripping away fat and creating two books on cooking "the slim way," I found that plate-sized tortillas formed a neat, fast, low-fat base for pizzas. I like to vary toppings to suit my pantry and whim. Roasted vegetables, such as eggplant, bell peppers and red onions, are other choices.

1 tablespoon olive oil
3 green onions, chopped
1 small zucchini, thinly sliced
¼ pound mushrooms, sliced
1 clove garlic, minced
3 ounces prosciutto, or 6 thin slices
 salami, cut into slivers
6 sun-dried tomatoes, diced, oil-packed
 or reconstituted if dried

Two 8-inch flour tortillas
2 tablespoons tomato paste or
 spaghetti sauce
2 teaspoons chopped fresh oregano,
 or ½ teaspoon dried
½ cup shredded Monterey Jack cheese
2 tablespoons freshly grated Romano
 cheese

Preheat the oven to 400°. In a skillet, heat the oil over medium-high heat. Add the onions, zucchini, mushrooms and garlic and sauté until glazed, about 2 to 3 minutes. Stir in the prosciutto or salami and the tomatoes and set aside.

Place the tortillas on a baking sheet and spread each tortilla with the tomato paste or sauce. Sprinkle with the oregano. Divide the vegetable mixture evenly between the tortillas and sprinkle with the cheeses. Bake for 6 to 8 minutes, or until the cheese is melted and the tortilla edges are lightly browned. Cut into wedges to serve.

Makes 2 Servings

Taco Pizza Pie

When I wrote *Vegetable Cookery* in the eighties, I styled this dish for a handsome color photograph. It makes a colorful, informal dinner entrée that is festive enough for guests. A platter salad of sliced jicama, red peppers, oranges and cucumbers is nice with guacamole for a starter. And for dessert, finish off with flan.

1½ cups all-purpose flour
½ cup yellow cornmeal
1 tablespoon baking powder
1 teaspoon salt
½ cup butter, cut into pieces
½ cup milk
1 pound lean ground pork or beef
1 clove garlic, minced
¼ teaspoon salt
¼ teaspoon ground cumin
½ teaspoon chili powder

1 can (4 ounces) chopped green chiles
1 cup cooked mashed pinto beans or black beans, or 1 can (8½ ounces) refried beans
2 medium tomatoes, chopped
3 green onions, chopped
⅓ cup coarsely chopped green bell pepper
1 cup shredded Monterey Jack cheese
1 cup shredded cheddar cheese

In a large bowl, mix together the flour, cornmeal, baking powder and salt. Add the butter and, with a pastry blender or fork, cut it in until the mixture resembles fine crumbs. Stir in the milk and mix until the dough forms a ball. Transfer the dough to a lightly floured work surface and knead until smooth, about 10 times. Roll the dough out into a 13-inch circle. Gently fold the dough into quarters and transfer it to an ungreased baking sheet or pizza pan. Unfold the dough and pinch the edge of the dough to form a 1-inch rim.

Preheat the oven to 400°. In a large skillet over medium heat, sauté the pork, garlic, salt, cumin and chili powder until browned and crumbly, about 4 to 5 minutes. Stir in the green chiles.

Spread the beans evenly over the dough and top with the meat mixture. Arrange the tomatoes in a circle around the edge of the pizza. Scatter the green onions in a circle inside the tomatoes and place the bell pepper in the center. Sprinkle with the cheeses. Bake for 20 minutes, or until the crust is golden brown on the edges.

Makes 4 to 6 Servings

Pasta & Grains

Fish & Poultry

Baked Fish and Vegetables Piraeus

Fish steaks and vegetables combine for a succulent full-meal entrée named after the Greek port of Piraeus. This was one of Yaya's (my Greek mother-in-law's) favorite dishes, which she baked in a big granite roasting pan.

3 tablespoons olive oil
1 large onion, chopped
2 stalks celery, or 1 small bulb fennel, chopped
3 small carrots, chopped
1 bunch green onions, chopped
1 bunch spinach, chopped
⅓ cup chopped fresh flat-leaf parsley

1 can (8 ounces) tomato sauce
2 cloves garlic, minced
2 tablespoons minced fresh basil
Salt and freshly ground black pepper to taste
2 pounds 1-inch-thick halibut or sea bass steaks
1 lemon, cut into wedges

In a large skillet, heat the oil over medium heat. Add the onion and sauté until soft. Add the celery or fennel, carrots and green onions and sauté until glazed. Add the spinach, parsley, tomato sauce, garlic, basil, salt and pepper, cover the skillet and simmer the mixture for 15 minutes.

Preheat the oven to 350°. Transfer one-half of the vegetable mixture to a greased 9-by-13-inch baking dish. Arrange the fish steaks over the vegetables and top with the remaining vegetables. Cover the pan and bake for 45 minutes, or until the fish flakes easily when tested with a fork. Serve with the lemon wedges.

Makes 6 Servings

Leek and Snapper Packets

I learned the trick of baking in parchment or foil in the seventies as I embarked on cooking in a healthier style. As fresh ginger became addictive, I included it in this easy-to-assemble-ahead entrée.

2 leeks
1 teaspoon olive oil
1½ teaspoons finely chopped fresh
  ginger
⅓ cup dry white wine
1 teaspoon grated lemon zest

12 ounces snapper or salmon fillet,
  cut into 2 pieces
Salt and freshly ground black pepper
  to taste
4 slices lemon
4 sprigs fresh flat-leaf parsley

Preheat the oven to 450°. Cut off and discard the green tops from the leeks and trim the root ends. Split the white part of the leeks lengthwise through the middle and wash thoroughly under cold running water; drain. Cut the white part of the leeks into 1¼-inch matchstick pieces.

In a large skillet, heat the oil over medium heat. Add the leeks and ginger and sauté until soft. Add the wine and lemon zest and cook until the liquid is reduced and forms a glaze on the vegetables.

Lay two 11-inch square sheets of aluminum foil or parchment paper on a work surface. Place the leek mixture in the center of each foil or parchment sheet, dividing evenly. Place a fish portion on top of each pile of leeks. Season the fish with salt and pepper and top with the lemon slices and parsley sprigs. Fold the foil or parchment over the food to completely enclose it, making a double fold in center and at both ends.

Place the packets on a baking sheet and bake for 8 to 10 minutes, or until the packets are puffed and the fish is just cooked through.

To serve, place a packet on each dinner plate and let the eaters open their own packets at the table.

Makes 2 Servings

Salmon Fillet with Fresh Herbs and Ginger

Salmon is my passion and I have prepared it all ways. Years ago as a camper, I even cooked it Indian fashion, staked to a cedar plank and grilled upright. I find this one of the easiest, most delectable entrées to serve guests.

1 salmon fillet, about 2½ pounds
2 tablespoons olive oil
2 teaspoons Dijon-style mustard
2 tablespoons lemon juice

1 tablespoon minced fresh ginger
2 teaspoons minced lemon zest
¼ cup mixed minced fresh flat-leaf
   parsley, chives, tarragon and dill

Preheat the broiler. Line a broiler pan with heavy-duty aluminum foil. Place the salmon on the broiler pan, skin-side down.

In a small bowl, mix together the olive oil, mustard, lemon juice, ginger, lemon zest and herbs. Spread the mustard mixture over the salmon fillet and let stand for 30 minutes.

Turn the salmon skin-side up and broil for 5 minutes. Peel off the skin (which can be charred), turn over the salmon and broil for 3 to 4 minutes, or until the salmon is cooked through.

Makes 6 Servings

Pickled Salmon and Red Onion Rings

A sojourn to Sweden in the sixties sold me on this excellent way with salmon. At a tour of the famed Operakelleren in Stockholm, the chef divulged the recipe. This spiced pickled fish, spooned from a crock, offers a tantalizing summer entrée for a picnic or patio meal. I also present it as an appetizer year-round. Accompany with rye or egg bread, sliced cucumbers and cherry tomatoes. You can substitute halibut for the salmon, if you wish.

2 pounds boneless salmon steaks or
   fillets
3 slices lemon
1 teaspoon salt
1 teaspoon mixed pickling spice,
   tied in a cheesecloth bag
1 bay leaf
1 medium-sized red onion, sliced and
   separated into rings

⅔ cup tarragon-flavored white wine
   vinegar
½ cup dry vermouth or white wine
6 whole allspice berries
6 whole peppercorns
3 tablespoons sugar
Minced fresh dill for garnish (optional)

Place the fish in a large saucepan and cover with water. Add the lemon, salt, pickling spice and bay leaf. Cover the saucepan and bring the mixture to a boil over high heat. Reduce the heat to low and simmer for 5 to 8 minutes, or until the fish flakes easily when tested with a fork. Drain the liquid from the fish and cool.

Remove any bones or skin from the fish and separate it along its natural seams into 1½-inch chunks. Place the fish and onion rings, alternating layers, in a 1½-quart jar or crock.

In a saucepan, combine the vinegar, vermouth or wine, allspice, peppercorns and sugar and bring to a boil over high heat. Reduce the heat to low and simmer until the sugar dissolves. Pour the hot vinegar mixture over the fish. Cover the jar or crock securely and chill for several hours or up to 2 to 3 days before serving. Serve garnished with dill, if desired.

Makes 8 Servings

Fish & Poultry

Chutney-Glazed Chicken

This was one of the first innovative ways I enhanced chicken breasts as a young career woman. Now I bone and skin the breasts so they acquire an appealing mahogany glaze while cooking. White and wild rice or couscous often accompanies them. For an attractive presentation, line a small custard cup with plastic wrap, spoon in each serving of rice or couscous, pat down and invert onto a plate; arrange the chicken alongside.

1½ tablespoons sweet-hot mustard
½ teaspoon curry powder
4 tablespoons mango chutney
4 teaspoons soy sauce
Salt and freshly ground black pepper
   to taste

4 boneless, skinless chicken breast
   halves, about 1½ pounds
1 mango, peeled and sliced
Watercress or arugula for garnish

Preheat the oven to 400°. In a bowl, mix together the mustard, curry powder, chutney, soy sauce, salt and pepper. Coat the chicken breasts with the mustard mixture and place them in an oiled baking pan. Bake for 12 to 15 minutes, or until cooked through.

About 2 minutes before the chicken is done, top it with the mango slices.

Serve garnished with watercress or arugula.

Makes 2 Servings

Chicken with Sun-Dried Tomatoes and Lemon

This dish receives accolades at my cooking classes. My home-cured olives that adorn it are imbued with lemon zest, garlic and rosemary.

1 tablespoon olive oil

1 large onion, chopped

4 cloves garlic, minced

4 boneless, skinless chicken breast halves, about 1½ pounds, lightly pounded to an even thickness

Salt and freshly ground black pepper to taste

½ cup dry white wine

⅓ cup chicken broth

½ lemon, thinly sliced and seeded

12 Mediterranean-style black olives, pitted if desired

⅓ cup slivered sun-dried tomatoes, oil-packed or reconstituted if dried

2 tablespoons slivered fresh arugula or basil leaves

Arugula or basil leaves for garnish

In a large skillet, heat the oil over medium heat. Add the onion and garlic and sauté for about 5 minutes, or until the onion is soft. Add the chicken, salt and pepper and sauté for 2 to 3 minutes, turning once, or until almost cooked through. Transfer the chicken and onion mixture to a plate and keep warm. Add the wine and broth to the pan and simmer for 2 minutes, until slightly reduced.

Return the chicken to the pan with the lemon slices, olives and tomatoes. Cover the pan and cook for 2 to 3 minutes, or until the chicken is cooked through.

Transfer the chicken to serving plates. Cook the remaining ingredients until the liquid is slightly reduced and syrupy. Spoon the pan juices, olives, tomatoes and lemon slices evenly over the chicken. Sprinkle with slivered arugula or basil and garnish with arugula or basil sprigs.

Makes 4 Servings

Chicken Breasts with Goat Cheese and Sun-Dried Tomatoes

This is a trendy dish from the eighties as California goat cheese and sun-dried tomatoes began to have wider market distribution. The piquant cheese and tart-sweet tomatoes interplay with grilled chicken for a gala, easy entrée.

4 boneless, skinless chicken breast halves, about 1½ pounds
3 tablespoons Dijon-style or stone-ground mustard
4 tablespoons lemon juice
2 tablespoons olive oil
1 tablespoon chopped fresh tarragon
1 tablespoon chopped fresh thyme
1 tablespoon chopped fresh chives
8 sun-dried tomatoes, oil-packed or reconstituted if dried
2 ounces chèvre (soft goat cheese)
8 leaves arugula for garnish

Place the chicken breasts in a shallow dish. In a small bowl, mix together the mustard, lemon juice, oil and herbs. Coat the chicken breasts with the mustard mixture and marinate for 1 hour.

Preheat the broiler. Place the chicken breasts on a foil-lined broiler pan and broil for 3 minutes, or until the top side is golden brown. Turn and broil the other side for 3 minutes. Place the chicken breasts in a 375° oven and bake for 7 to 8 minutes, or until cooked through. Add the tomatoes during the last few minutes of baking, just to heat them through.

Arrange the chicken breasts and tomatoes on serving plates, top with the cheese and garnish with the arugula leaves.

Makes 4 Servings

Fish & Poultry

Five-Spice Roasted Chicken

Always on the lookout for a new taste treat, I found Chinese five-spice powder met this criteria as I pursued ethnic cooking around the world. Cinnamon, star anise and cloves dominate this sultry spice blend, available in an Asian market or good supermarket. For an East-West menu, accompany with roasted yams and red onions and napa cabbage slaw. Savor candied ginger ice cream and sesame cookies for dessert.

1 broiler-fryer chicken, about 3½ pounds
Salt and freshly ground black pepper to taste
1 teaspoon Chinese five-spice powder

2 tablespoons soy sauce
2 tablespoons dry sherry
1 teaspoon chopped fresh ginger
2 cloves garlic, minced
2 teaspoons Asian sesame oil

Preheat the oven to 425°. Remove the internal organs and extra fat from the chicken. Rinse the chicken well, inside and out, under cold running water and pat dry with paper towels. Season the chicken with salt, pepper and five-spice powder and place on a rack in a roasting pan. Roast the chicken for 15 minutes.

In a bowl, mix together the soy sauce, sherry, ginger, garlic and sesame oil and brush one-half of the mixture over the chicken. Reduce the oven heat to 375° and roast the chicken for about 1 hour longer, basting occasionally with the remaining soy sauce mixture, until the temperature of the thickest part of the breast meat registers 170° when tested with an instant-read thermometer and the drumstick moves easily.

Let the chicken stand for 15 minutes before carving it into serving pieces.

Makes 4 to 6 Servings

Roasted Chicken and Spuds

A plump, golden bird makes an easy, succulent entrée anytime. In summer, roast it in advance and savor it chilled, or sliced or diced in a salad. This was a weekly staple dish when I was cooking for our family of six.

1 broiler-fryer chicken, about 3½ pounds	8 cloves garlic, minced
Sea salt and freshly ground black pepper to taste	3 to 4 fresh rosemary sprigs
	2 to 3 pounds small potatoes, such as red creamer or Yukon gold
Juice of ½ lemon	¼ cup olive oil

Remove the internal organs and extra fat from the chicken. Rinse the chicken well, inside and out, under cold running water and pat dry with paper towels. Season the chicken with salt and pepper and sprinkle with lemon juice.

With your fingers, gently separate the chicken skin from the meat. Place the garlic cloves under the skin and inside the cavity of the chicken. Tuck the rosemary sprigs inside the chicken's cavity. Place the chicken breast-side up on a rack in a large roasting pan and let stand at room temperature for 30 minutes.

Preheat the oven to 450°. Roast the chicken for 20 minutes.

While the chicken is roasting, toss the potatoes in a bowl with the oil. Reduce the oven heat to 375°. Add the potatoes to the pan with the chicken and continue to roast for 30 to 40 more minutes longer, or until the temperature of the thickest part of the breast meat registers 170° when tested with an instant-read thermometer and the drumstick moves easily.

Let the chicken stand for 15 minutes before carving it into serving pieces. Serve it with the potatoes.

Makes 4 to 6 Servings

Smoked Barbecued Turkey with Gingered Cranberry Relish

For the Thanksgiving holiday, this is my favorite way to cook the bird while the stuffing oven-bakes along with yams and red onions. Then, I place the turkey on a carving board, strew it with garlands of rosemary and garnish it with zigzag-cut lemons. The fresh, tangy cranberry relish is superb with barbecued meats or chicken. Add sugar to taste; I like it on the tart side.

1 turkey, 20 to 22 pounds
Salt and freshly ground black pepper
   to taste
6 cloves garlic, minced

1 onion, quartered
1 orange, sliced
Gingered Cranberry Relish, follows

Remove the innards and extra fat from the turkey. Rinse the turkey well, inside and out, under cold running water and pat dry with paper towels. Season the turkey well with salt and pepper.

With your fingers, gently separate the turkey skin from the meat. Place the garlic cloves under the skin of the turkey. Slip the onion and orange inside the cavity.

Ignite about 30 briquettes in a barbecue with a cover and let them burn down.

Place the turkey in a foil pan and insert a meat thermometer in the thickest part of a thigh. Place the pan on the grill and cook over fairly low heat with the grill covered, until the meat thermometer reads 175°, about 3½ to 4 hours.

Let the turkey stand for 15 to 20 minutes before carving and serve with Gingered Cranberry Relish.

Makes 16 Servings

Gingered Cranberry Relish

2 oranges
2 Granny Smith apples
1 package (12 ounces) whole
   cranberries

1 tablespoon chopped fresh ginger
⅓ to ½ cup sugar

With a vegetable peeler, remove the zest from the oranges, avoiding the bitter white pith; set aside. Peel off and discard the white pith that remains on the outside of the oranges and cut the oranges into sixths. Quarter and core the apples.

In a food processor workbowl, combine ½ each of the oranges, orange zest, apples, cranberries, ginger and sugar and process until finely chopped. Transfer the mixture to a bowl. Repeat the chopping process with the remaining half of the ingredients, transfer to the bowl and mix well. Cover the bowl and chill the relish for at least 4 hours, or up to 3 to 4 days before serving.

Makes 5 Cups

Meats

Balsamic Steak and Red Onions

A visit to the Fini production cellars of balsamic vinegar in Modena, Italy, prompted me into the joys of cooking with this intriguing ingredient. Here as a finishing sauce for steak, it enhances natural flavors. Serve the dish hot, or let it cool, and use it to top a salad of mixed greens tossed with vinaigrette.

¼ cup balsamic vinegar
3 tablespoons olive oil
1 tablespoon minced fresh rosemary
2 teaspoons minced fresh thyme
3 cloves garlic, minced
Salt and freshly ground black pepper
   to taste

2 medium-sized red onions,
   cut into ½-inch wedges
1 flank steak, about 1½ pounds
Arugula leaves, or flat-leaf parsley
   sprigs for garnish

In a bowl, mix together the vinegar, oil, rosemary, thyme, garlic, salt and pepper and brush about 2 tablespoons of the mixture over the onions.

Place the remaining vinegar mixture in a baking dish. Add the steak to the dish and turn to coat both sides. Marinate meat and onions for 1 hour or longer.

Preheat the broiler. Place the meat and onions on a broiling pan and broil for about 2 to 3 minutes per side for medium-rare meats.

Slice the meat thinly on the diagonal and arrange in a fan shape on each serving plate with the onions alongside. Garnish with arugula leaves or sprigs of flat-leaf parsley.

Makes 6 Servings

Meats

Flank Steak Teriyaki

This is a favorite from the fifties and a dish that launched Asian cooking for me. The marinade grills to a mahogany sheen on flank steak for a winning entrée for family or guests, any season. Grill red onion rings alongside for a flavorful companion. Leftover meat strips can embellish a green salad or fill a pita pocket or whole-grain bread for a sandwich the next day.

3 tablespoons soy sauce
2 tablespoons honey
1½ tablespoons red wine vinegar
2 cloves garlic, minced
2 teaspoons minced fresh ginger

1 green onion (white part only), chopped
About 1½ pounds flank steak or top sirloin

In a shallow pan, mix together the soy sauce, honey, vinegar, garlic, ginger and onion. Add the steak to the pan and turn to coat both sides with the marinade. Cover the dish and refrigerate for several hours or overnight, turning once or twice.

Let the meat stand at room temperature for 30 minutes before cooking.

Preheat the boiler or grill. Broil or grill the meat about 4 inches from the heat source for about 4 minutes on each side for medium-rare meat. Slice the meat thinly on the diagonal to serve.

Some health authorities discourage eating undercooked meat because of possible bacterial contamination.

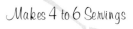

Makes 4 to 6 Servings

Meats

Beef Stifado

Lightly toasted whole cinnamon imbues meat with a marvelous spicy flavor as it slow cooks in this classic Greek entrée. This is an excellent dish to make in advance and reheat for a party occasion. Accompany with a tomato and cucumber salad strewn with feta cheese and Mediterranean-style olives. If you prefer, 6 to 8 chicken thighs can substitute for the beef; allow 45 minutes to 1 hour for total cooking time.

1 tablespoon olive oil	¾ cup dry red wine
2 pounds lean beef stew meat, cut into 1½-inch pieces	3 tablespoons red wine vinegar
One 2-inch stick cinnamon	3 tablespoons tomato paste
Salt and freshly ground black pepper to taste	1 tablespoon brown sugar
3 cloves garlic, minced	1½ pounds small whole onions
1½ teaspoons mixed pickling spice, tied in a cheesecloth bag	2 tablespoons dried currants (optional)
	2 tablespoons minced fresh flat-leaf parsley

In a large skillet, heat the oil over medium-high heat. Add the beef and cinnamon stick and cook until all sides of the meat are browned.

Season the meat with salt and pepper and add the garlic. Add the pickling spice, wine, vinegar, tomato paste and brown sugar and mix well. Cover the skillet and simmer for 1 hour.

Peel the onions and cut a small cross in the root end of each to prevent them from bursting. Add the onions and currants, if using, to the skillet and simmer for 30 minutes longer, or until the onions and meat are tender.

Remove the cinnamon stick and pickling spices before serving. Sprinkle servings with parsley.

Makes 6 to 8 Servings

Mom's Meat Loaf

This long-time favorite is good either hot or cold, sandwiched between slices of chewy whole wheat or country-style bread.

1½ pounds lean ground beef,
   or 1 pound ground beef and
   ½ pound ground pork
⅔ cup soft sourdough French
   breadcrumbs
1 small onion, chopped
1 teaspoon salt
¼ teaspoon black pepper

2 eggs, beaten
¾ cup milk
1 teaspoon dry mustard
2 tablespoons balsamic vinegar
⅓ cup ketchup
1½ teaspoons Dijon-style mustard
2 tablespoons packed brown sugar
½ teaspoon Worcestershire sauce

Preheat the oven to 350°. In a bowl, combine the ground meat, breadcrumbs, onion, salt, pepper, eggs, milk, mustard and vinegar. Shape the meat mixture into a 7-by-12-inch loaf and place in a 9-by-13-inch baking pan. Bake for 1 hour.

In a bowl, mix together the ketchup, mustard, brown sugar and Worcestershire. Spread the mixture over the top of the meat loaf. Return the meat loaf to the oven and bake for an additional 15 minutes, or until cooked through.

Makes 8 Servings

Meats

Joe's Special with Mushrooms

An old-time specialty from New Joe's North Beach Italian Restaurant in San Francisco gets an update with mushrooms. This scramble of ground meat, spinach and eggs is a good choice for a spur-of-the-moment entrée. In the fifties, as a young career woman, I prepared it often for my boss at *Sunset* magazine. For a vegetarian-style entrée, replace the meat with portobello mushrooms, thinly sliced and sautéed.

1 tablespoon olive oil
1 small red onion, chopped
¼ pound small white mushrooms, sliced
1 pound lean ground lamb, beef or turkey
2 cloves garlic, minced
Salt and freshly ground black pepper to taste

1 bunch spinach, finely chopped
2 eggs
1 tablespoon chopped fresh oregano or sage
2 tablespoons freshly grated Romano or Parmesan cheese

In a large skillet, heat the oil over medium-high heat. Add the onion and mushrooms and sauté them until soft. Push the vegetables to the sides of the pan. Add the ground meat, garlic, salt and pepper and cook until the meat is browned and crumbly. Add the spinach and cook for 2 minutes, or just until the spinach wilts.

Break the eggs into the skillet and cook, stirring, until mixed and cooked through. Sprinkle servings with the oregano or sage and cheese.

Makes 3 to 4 Servings

Mexican Taco Casserole

This spicy dish with decorative toppings stems from the sixties when a big pitcher of sangria was a standard accompaniment. Hot rolled tortillas were passed in a basket and a fresh fruit platter of pineapple spears, honeydew melon wedges and strawberries composed dessert.

1 tablespoon olive oil
2 medium onions, finely chopped
One 2-inch cinnamon stick
2 pounds lean ground pork, or
   1 pound each ground pork and
   ground turkey
2 cloves garlic, minced
2 cans (8 ounces each) tomato sauce
2 tablespoons red wine vinegar
½ teaspoon ground cumin
½ teaspoon chili powder
½ teaspoon dried oregano

½ teaspoon ground allspice
Salt and freshly ground black pepper
   to taste
1 can (1 pound) dark kidney beans,
   rinsed and drained
1 package (6 ounces) small corn chips
2 cups shredded Monterey Jack cheese
2 green onions, chopped
Leaves from 1 bunch fresh cilantro,
   chopped
¾ cup plain yogurt or sour cream

In a large skillet, heat the oil over medium heat. Add the onions and cinnamon stick and sauté until the onions are soft. Add the ground meat and sauté until browned and crumbly. Stir in the garlic, tomato sauce, vinegar, cumin, chili powder, oregano, allspice, salt and pepper. Cover the skillet and simmer for 30 minutes. Remove and discard cinnamon stick. Stir in the beans.

Preheat the oven to 375°. Place one-third of the corn chips in a layer in a greased 2-quart casserole. Sprinkle with one-third of the cheese. Cover the cheese with one-half of the meat sauce. Top with another one-third of the corn chips, one-third of the cheese and the remaining half of the meat sauce. Top with the remaining corn chips and cheese. (If desired, your can refrigerate the casserole at this point until serving time.)

Bake the casserole for 20 minutes (40 minutes, if refrigerated), or until heated through.

In a bowl, toss the onions and cilantro together. Make a border around the edge of the casserole with the onion-cilantro mixture and spoon the yogurt into the center.

Makes 8 to 10 Servings

Meats

Lamb Bandit Style

This easy-to-assemble entrée brings an aura of surprise to the table. In Greek tradition, the meat and vegetables are sealed and cooked in paper—"bandit style." For a charming first course, start with stuffed grape leaves and Greek olives. This dish was inspired when I wrote a Greek cookbook in the sixties, and ever since I have enjoyed other variations, such as a paper bag of sausages, sliced potatoes and green onions.

2 round-bone lamb chops, about
   8 ounces each
Salt and freshly ground black pepper
   to taste
2 teaspoons fresh oregano leaves, or
   ½ teaspoon dried, crumbled
1 clove garlic, minced

2 small zucchini, halved lengthwise
2 small yellow squash, halved
   lengthwise
2 green onions, chopped
1 ounce feta cheese, crumbled
1½ tablespoons lemon juice
1 tablespoon olive oil

Preheat the oven to 350°. Place 2 white paper lunch bags on a work surface and grease the insides well. Season the chops with salt, pepper, oregano and garlic. Place one chop in each of the bags. Top the chops with the zucchini and yellow squash, dividing evenly. Top with the onions and crumbled cheese. Drizzle with the lemon juice and oil.

Cut off 3 inches from the tops of the bags. Close the bags and fold the tops down a few times; secure with paper clips. Place the packets in a baking pan and bake for 1 hour. To serve, place the sealed packets on dinner plates and let the eaters open the packets at the table.

Makes 2 Servings

Lamb Shanks Cacciatore

In a family-run Florentine trattoria along the Arno, this was one of the daily regional dishes on a visit in the seventies. A rich brown gravy evolves during cooking, just right for spooning over a pilaf or polenta accompaniment.

2 tablespoons olive oil
4 lamb shanks
1 medium onion, finely chopped
Salt and freshly ground black pepper
   to taste
2 cloves garlic, minced
1 cup dry red wine

1 can (10½ ounces) consommé
3 tablespoons tomato paste
1 carrot, finely chopped
4 anchovy fillets, chopped
2 tablespoons cornstarch
2 tablespoons cold water

Preheat the oven to 375°. In a large rimmed skillet, heat the oil over medium heat. Add the lamb and cook, turning, until both sides are browned. Add the onion and sauté until limp. Season the lamb and onion with salt and pepper and add the garlic, wine, consommé, tomato paste, carrot and anchovy fillets. Cover the skillet and bake for 2 hours, or until meat is tender when pierced with a fork. Transfer the meat to a platter and keep warm.

Bring the cooking juices to a boil on the stovetop. In a small cup, mix the cornstarch with the water and add it to the skillet. Cook, stirring constantly, until thickened. Arrange the lamb portions on serving plates and pass the sauce in a bowl to spoon over the lamb.

Makes 4 Servings

Meats

Lamb Shish Kabob

Touring the Greek islands, I found this dish ubiquitous on every menu, but the best version is still done at home. This is ideal for any season, indoors or out. For accompaniments, consider bulgur pilaf, cucumbers in yogurt, *dolmathes* (stuffed grape leaves) and fresh fruit with baklava or almond cake.

1 cup dry red wine
3 tablespoons lemon juice
3 tablespoons olive oil
Salt and freshly ground black pepper
   to taste
2 teaspoons chopped fresh oregano,
   or ½ teaspoon dried
3 cloves garlic, minced
1 small onion, sliced

2 pounds boneless leg of lamb,
   cut into 1½-inch squares
Bay leaves
1 red bell pepper, cut into 1½-inch
   squares
1 medium-sized red onion, cut into
   1½-inch chunks
Lemon wedges for garnish

In a bowl, mix together the wine, lemon juice, oil, salt, pepper, oregano, garlic and sliced onion. Add the meat to the bowl, turning several times to coat it with the marinade. Cover the bowl and refrigerate it overnight.

Prepare a medium-hot barbecue fire.

On metal or soaked bamboo skewers, alternate chunks of lamb, bay leaves, pepper chunks and onion chunks. Cook the skewers over hot coals, basting with the marinade and turning once, for about 20 minutes. Garnish each serving with a lemon wedge.

Variation: Skewered Lamb, Stuffed Grape Leaves and Cherry Tomatoes

Omit the vegetables and grill only skewers of meat. Accompany with skewers of cold canned stuffed grape leaves (dolmathes) and cherry tomatoes, alternating them on additional skewers.

Makes 6 Servings

Meats

Roasted Portobellos and Pork Balsamic

Since portobello mushrooms burst into the marketplace of late, I incorporated them into this long-time way with chops.

¼ cup dry sherry
3 tablespoons balsamic vinegar
2 cloves garlic, minced
1 shallot, chopped
2 tablespoons mixed minced fresh
   flat-leaf parsley, thyme or sage,
   and rosemary

2 tablespoons plus 1 teaspoon olive oil
2 large portobello mushroom caps
4 boneless pork loin chops,
   about 1 pound
2 tablespoons Dijon-style mustard

In a small saucepan, bring the sherry to a boil and cook until reduced by half. Remove it from the heat and add the vinegar, garlic, shallot, herbs and 2 tablespoons oil.

Place the mushrooms in a shallow glass dish and add one-half of the vinegar mixture. Spread the pork chops with a thin coating of Dijonnaise and place them in another shallow dish. Cover the pork with the remaining vinegar mixture. Marinate the mushrooms and pork chops for at least 30 minutes.

Preheat the oven to 425°. Transfer the mushrooms to a baking pan and roast them for 10 to 15 minutes, until cooked through. Remove them from the oven and keep them warm.

Heat the broiler. In an ovenproof skillet, heat the 1 teaspoon oil over medium heat. Add the pork chops and brown the underside of the meat. Slip the pork chops under the broiler and cook until the top is browned and the meat is cooked through, about 2 to 3 minutes. Slice the mushrooms and place them on top of the meat on serving plates.

Makes 4 Servings

Meats

Gingered Pork Loin with Pistachios

In the sixties this dish seemed avant-garde, with green peppercorns, pistachios and ginger adding pizzazz.

2 pounds boneless pork loin
3 cloves garlic, minced
2 teaspoons green peppercorns
⅓ cup pistachio nuts
⅓ cup golden raisins
3 tablespoons Dijon-style mustard

1½ tablespoons soy sauce
1½ teaspoons chopped fresh ginger
2 teaspoons grated lemon zest
Arugula or flat-leaf parsley sprigs
   for garnish
Lime or lemon wedges for garnish

Preheat the oven to 325°. Lay the pork flat on a work surface and sprinkle it with one-half of the garlic, the peppercorns, pistachios and raisins.

Starting from the long side, roll up the pork around the filling and tie it securely with a kitchen string.

In a bowl, mix together the mustard, soy sauce, ginger, lemon zest and the remaining half of the garlic and spread it over the surface of the pork. Place the pork roll in a roasting pan, insert a meat thermometer into the center and roast for about 45 to 50 minutes, until the thermometer reads 160°. Transfer the pork to a platter. Cut the pork into slices and serve it hot or cold, garnished with arugula or parsley and citrus wedges.

Makes 8 Servings

Pork Chops Provençal

Having enjoyed many trips to the Provence region of France, I have recreated the memorable flavors in this favorite fast way with pork.

4 center-cut pork chops,
   boneless if desired
2 tablespoons olive oil
2 tablespoons mixed minced fresh
   sage, thyme and flat-leaf parsley
2 cloves garlic, minced
1 large shallot, chopped

½ cup dry vermouth or white wine
½ cup chicken broth
8 sun-dried tomato halves, oil-packed
   or reconstituted if dried
4 to 6 slices lemon
8 salt-cured black olives, pitted
Minced fresh flat-leaf parsley, sage or

Rub the pork chops with 1 tablespoon of the oil and the herbs and garlic. Place the chops on a plate and marinate for 1 hour.

In a large skillet, heat the remaining 1 tablespoon oil over medium heat. Add the pork chops and the shallot and cook until browned on both sides. Add the vermouth or wine with the broth, tomatoes, lemon and olives. Cover the skillet and simmer for 15 to 20 minutes, or until the pork is tender and cooked through. Garnish servings with the

Makes 4 Servings

Moussaka

This classic Greek entrée has countless variations. Besides eggplant, zucchini, potatoes and mushrooms are appealing ingredients, or use a combination of two or more. A vegetarian version is another option. The casserole can also be baked in small eggplant boats for compact individual servings.

1 tablespoon olive oil
2 large onions, finely chopped
2 pounds ground lamb, beef or turkey, or a combination of 2 meats
¼ cup tomato paste
1 cup dry red wine
2 cloves garlic, minced
1 tablespoon cinnamon
1 teaspoon ground allspice
Salt and freshly ground black pepper to taste
2 tablespoons minced fresh flat-leaf parsley

2 large eggplants
¼ cup butter
¼ cup flour
3 cups milk
4 ounces feta cheese
Salt and freshly ground black pepper to taste
¼ teaspoon nutmeg
4 eggs
⅓ cup fine dry breadcrumbs
1 cup freshly grated Romano or Parmesan cheese

In a large skillet, heat the oil over medium heat. Add the onions and sauté until soft. Add the meat and cook until browned and crumbly. Stir in the tomato paste, wine, garlic, cinnamon, allspice, salt, pepper and parsley. Cover the skillet and simmer for 45 minutes, or until the sauce is thick and the flavors are blended.

Preheat the oven to 400°. Cut the eggplants into ¾-inch-thick slices. Place the eggplant slices on 2 generously oiled 10-by-15-inch baking pans and turn to coat both sides of the eggplant slices with the oil. Cover the pan loosely with foil and bake for 30 minutes, or until the eggplant is tender, turning once.

In a saucepan, melt the butter over medium-low heat and blend in the flour; gradually stir in the milk and cook, stirring, until thickened. Crumble the feta cheese into the saucepan and season with salt, pepper and nutmeg. In a bowl, beat the eggs until light and blend the hot sauce into them.

Preheat the oven to 350°. Arrange one-half of the eggplant slices in a layer in a large baking pan. Mix the meat sauce with the breadcrumbs and spread one-half of the mixture over the eggplant in the baking pan. Sprinkle with one-half of the grated cheese. Top the cheese with the remaining half of the eggplant and the remaining meat sauce. Spoon the white sauce over the top and sprinkle with the remaining half of the cheese.

Bake for 50 minutes, or until the custard sauce is set and lightly browned. Let the casserole stand for 10 to 15 minutes. Cut into squares to serve.

Variation: Zucchini Moussaka

Instead of eggplant, substitute 2 pounds zucchini, cut lengthwise or on the diagonal into ⅓-inch-thick slices. Sauté the zucchini in olive oil, turning, until tender-crisp. Continue with the basic moussaka recipe.

Variation: Potato Moussaka

Instead of eggplant, substitute 2 pounds Yukon gold potatoes, peeled and cut into ¼-inch-thick slices. Sauté the potato slices in olive oil until golden brown. Continue with the basic moussaka recipe.

Variation: Mushroom Moussaka

Instead of eggplant, substitute 2 pounds brown mushrooms, sliced. Sauté the mushrooms in olive oil just until soft and glazed. Continue with the basic moussaka recipe.

Makes 8 to 10 Servings

Moussaka

Vegetables

Mustard- and Brown Sugar-Glazed Carrots

As my dear artist friend, Mary Tift, and I savored many luncheons in her working studio alongside San Francisco Bay, food was most often the cornerstone of our conversation. She could transform even the humble carrot into a queenly dish.

6 to 8 large carrots, sliced on the
   diagonal
2 tablespoons butter
1 tablespoon Dijon-style mustard
1 tablespoon brown sugar, packed

Salt and freshly ground black pepper
   to taste
Chopped fresh chives, flat-leaf parsley
   or dill for garnish

In a saucepan, cook the carrots in a small amount of boiling salted water until tender, about 6 to 8 minutes; drain well. Add the butter, mustard, sugar, salt and pepper to the saucepan and stir gently to coat. Cook the carrots over medium heat until glazed. Sprinkle with the chives, parsley or dill and serve hot.

Makes 6 to 8 Servings

Ratatouille with Basil

An abundance of fresh basil and pistachios lends a bright accent to this traditional Provençal stew. Excellent hot or cold, it makes a fine accompaniment to grilled fare. Or, for a vegetarian meal, offer a green salad with goat cheese, fougasse or foccacia and polenta wedges. Finish with a fruit platter.

¼ cup olive oil

2 red bell peppers, seeded and cut into 1-inch pieces

2 yellow onions, sliced

1 medium eggplant, cut in half lengthwise, halves cut into ½-inch-thick slices

½ pound white or brown mushrooms, halved or quartered (optional)

4 zucchini, cut into ½-inch-thick slices

3 cloves garlic, minced

¼ cup minced fresh flat-leaf parsley

Salt and freshly ground black pepper to taste

3 large tomatoes, peeled and cut into ½-inch pieces

½ cup chopped fresh basil

3 tablespoons chopped pistachio nuts

In a large Dutch oven or saucepan, heat the oil over medium heat. Add the peppers and onions and sauté until soft, about 10 minutes. Stir in the eggplant, mushrooms, if using, zucchini, garlic, parsley, salt and pepper. Cover and cook over medium heat for about 25 minutes, stirring occasionally. Add the tomatoes and cook for 10 to 15 minutes longer, basting with the vegetable juices.

Serve the ratatouille hot or cold, sprinkled with basil and pistachio nuts.

Makes 8 Servings

Vegetables

Roasted Vegetables with Pesto

Roasting vegetables gives them a caramelized goodness that is excellent hot or cold. When I developed a pesto cookbook in the nineties, I discovered that a range of different herb pestos enhanced this dish. My favorites were sun-dried tomato and basil pestos.

6 small red-skinned potatoes
2 small Japanese eggplants
2 medium zucchini
¼ pound white mushrooms, about
   1½ inches in diameter
2 tablespoons extra virgin olive oil

2 tablespoons balsamic vinegar
Salt and freshly ground black pepper
   to taste
Sun-Dried Tomato Pesto, page 20,
   or Basil Pesto, page 51, for
   accompaniment

Preheat the oven to 475°. Cut the potatoes into ½-inch-thick slices. Cut the eggplants and zucchini on the diagonal into ½-inch-thick slices. Cut the mushrooms in half. Place the vegetables in a bowl with the oil and vinegar and marinate for a few minutes. Season with salt and pepper.

Place the marinated vegetables in a single layer in a baking pan and roast for 20 minutes, turning once or twice until all of the vegetables are cooked. Accompany the vegetables with pesto to spoon over the top.

Makes 4 to 6 Servings

Sherried Mushrooms

Slathering mushrooms in heavy cream was my passion in the sixties. Now, as less is often better, a splash of balsamic vinegar and sherry lend the accent along with herbs.

1 tablespoon olive oil or butter
1 clove garlic, minced
1 shallot, chopped
½ pound small white or brown
   mushrooms (See Note)
1 teaspoon chopped fresh tarragon,
   or ¼ teaspoon dried

3 tablespoons dry sherry
1 tablespoon balsamic vinegar
Salt and freshly ground black pepper
   to taste
2 tablespoons minced fresh flat-leaf
   parsley

In a large skillet, heat the oil or butter over medium heat. Add the garlic, shallot and mushrooms and sauté until glazed, about 1 to 2 minutes. Add the tarragon, sherry, vinegar, salt and pepper and sauté very quickly until the juices are reduced. Sprinkle with parsley and serve hot.

Note: In place of the white or brown mushrooms, you can also use ½ pound sliced stemmed oyster or portobello mushrooms.

Makes 2 to 4 Servings

Vegetables

Spinach and Mushroom Phyllo Pastry

Greek *spanakopita*, spinach-filled pastry appetizers, inspired this fat roll of golden-brown vegetable pastry. It is novel paired with broiled salmon fillets or grilled shrimp bathed with garlic oil. Sometimes I add a few leaves of chopped Swiss chard cut from my kitchen garden to augment the spinach.

1 tablespoon olive oil
1 large white or yellow onion, finely
  chopped
1 bunch green onions, chopped, or
  1 leek (white part only), chopped
¼ pound white or brown mushrooms,
  chopped
1 bunch spinach, stems removed
¼ cup chopped fresh flat-leaf parsley

⅛ teaspoon freshly ground nutmeg
Salt and freshly ground black pepper
  to taste
3 eggs, beaten
¼ cup freshly grated Parmesan cheese
¼ cup shredded Gruyère cheese
¼ cup shredded Emmentaler cheese
5 sheets phyllo dough
2 tablespoons unsalted butter, melted

Preheat the oven to 375°. In a large skillet, heat the oil over medium heat. Add the onion and green onions or leek and sauté until the vegetables are limp. Add the mushrooms and cook until glazed. Add the spinach and cook until it is just barely wilted. Remove the skillet from the heat, drain off any extra liquid and cool.

Add the parsley, nutmeg, salt, pepper, eggs and cheeses to the cooked vegetable mixture and mix well.

Lay 1 sheet of phyllo on a work surface and brush lightly with melted butter. Top with a second sheet of phyllo and brush lightly with butter. Repeat the layering process with the remaining sheets of phyllo, brushing with butter between layers. Spoon the spinach mixture in a strip along one long side of the phyllo. Fold the short ends of the phyllo over by 1 inch and roll up the dough, encasing the spinach filling securely.

Place the roll seam-side down on a lightly buttered baking sheet. Bake for 40 minutes, or until crisp and browned. Cut the roll into 2-inch slices and serve warm.

Makes 6 Servings

Vegetables

Asparagus and Eggs, Italian-Style

I remember my father would daily bring home a tidy boxful of the day's produce and staples when I was a child. The spring bounty featured "grass," as that was the grocers' term for asparagus. It was served simply boiled with drawn butter. Later, in the seventies, I discovered this fast, chic way of serving asparagus in Italy.

¾ pound asparagus
1 tablespoon butter
2 eggs
Salt and freshly ground black pepper
   to taste

3 ounces thinly sliced prosciutto or
   ham, cut into strips (see *Note*)
¼ cup freshly grated Parmesan or
   Romano cheese

Preheat the oven to 350°. Trim the ends from the asparagus and discard; cook the asparagus in boiling salted water until tender, about 5 to 7 minutes; drain.

Divide the butter betweem 2 small ramekins and place them in the oven until the butter is melted.

Break an egg into each ramekin and sprinkle with salt and pepper. Bake until the egg whites are just barely set, about 7 minutes.

Arrange the asparagus and prosciutto over the eggs, dividing evenly, and sprinkle with the cheese. Continue to bake until the cheese melts, about 2 minutes longer.

Note: If desired, replace the prosciutto with ¼ pound of small cooked shrimp.

Makes 2 Servings

Spinach Frittata

This dish became a favorite entertaining side dish to accompany garlicky roast lamb or flank steak when I was a new bride. There was no fear of scorching the vegetables, as it oven-baked and could be assembled ahead. Cartwheels of tomato brighten this green "pie."

1 bunch spinach, stems removed
1 bunch green onions, chopped
½ cup plain yogurt
2 eggs
Salt and freshly ground black pepper
   to taste

2 teaspoons minced fresh tarragon,
   or ½ teaspoon dried
3 tablespoons minced fresh flat-leaf
   parsley
¼ cup freshly grated Parmesan cheese
1 large tomato, thinly sliced

Preheat the oven to 350°. Heat a large skillet over medium-high heat. Add the spinach and onions and sauté for 1 minute, until the spinach is barely limp. Transfer the mixture to a food processor workbowl or blender container and cool slightly. Add the yogurt, eggs, salt, pepper, tarragon, parsley and 2 tablespoons of the cheese and process until the vegetables are minced. Transfer the mixture to a greased 9-inch pie pan.

Arrange the tomato slices decoratively on top of the spinach mixture and sprinkle with the remaining 2 tablespoons of the cheese. Bake for 25 to 30 minutes, or until the eggs are set. Cut into wedges to serve.

Makes 6 Servings

Stuffed Eggplant Boats

On several trips to Turkey, I have found the cuisine captivating. This is a sample of one discovery. Slender six-inch eggplants make neat individual servings for this spicy entrée.

8 small eggplants, about 6 inches long
Salt
3 large tomatoes, peeled and chopped
1 tablespoon olive oil
1 large onion, chopped
1 pound lean ground lamb or turkey
2 tablespoons minced fresh flat-leaf
   parsley

Freshly ground black pepper to taste
2 cloves garlic, minced
½ teaspoon ground allspice
½ cup freshly grated Parmesan cheese
1 can (8 ounces) tomato sauce

Preheat the oven to 400°. With a knife, slit the eggplants lengthwise to within 1 inch of each stem end. Sprinkle salt lightly into the slits and let the eggplants stand for 15 minutes. Rinse the eggplants under cold running water and pat dry with paper towels. Place the eggplants in a baking dish, cover with foil and bake for 30 minutes. Reduce the oven heat to 375°.

Peel and chop 2 of the tomatoes. In a large skillet, heat the oil over medium heat and sauté the onion until golden. Add the ground meat and cook until browned and crumbly. Add the chopped tomatoes, parsley, salt to taste, pepper, garlic and allspice. Cover the skillet and simmer the mixture for 15 minutes. Remove the skillet from the heat and cool slightly.

Pack the meat mixture into the slits of the eggplants and place them in a baking dish. Cut the remaining tomato into wedges and arrange on top of the eggplants. Sprinkle the eggplant boats with the cheese and pour the tomato sauce over the top. Cover the dish with aluminum foil and bake for 45 minutes.

Heat the broiler. Remove the foil from the baking dish and broil the eggplant boats for about 1 minute, or until the top is lightly browned. Serve hot or at room temperature.

Makes 4 Servings

 Vegetables

Swiss Chard, Sun-Dried Tomato and Sausage Stuffing

This was a hit at last year's Thanksgiving. The old-time Italian recipe got an update with sun-dried tomatoes, fresh basil and cheese. It's also a choice complement to grilled pork chops.

6 to 7 cups day-old sourdough bread
   cubes
2 eggs
1½ cups chicken broth
1 tablespoon olive oil
2 leeks, chopped
1 bunch Swiss chard, chopped
1 stalk celery, finely chopped
1 pound ground pork sausage

¾ teaspoon salt
3 tablespoons chopped fresh basil
1 tablespoon minced fresh sage,
   or ¾ teaspoon dried
1 tablespoon minced fresh rosemary
½ cup minced fresh flat-leaf parsley
1 cup slivered sun-dried tomatoes, oil-
   packed or reconstituted if dried
¾ cup grated Romano cheese

Preheat the oven to 325°. Grease a 9-by-13-inch baking pan.

Place the bread on a baking sheet and bake until lightly toasted, about 20 minutes, shaking occasionally.

In a large bowl, beat the eggs until blended and stir in the broth. Add the toasted bread cubes and toss to coat.

In a large skillet, heat the oil over medium heat and sauté the leeks until soft. Add the chard and celery and sauté for 2 minutes. Transfer the vegetable mixture to the bowl with the bread.

Add the sausage to the skillet and sauté until browned and crumbly. Mix in the salt, basil, sage, rosemary, parsley and tomatoes. Transfer the meat mixture to the bowl with the vegetables. Add one-half of the cheese and mix well. Transfer the stuffing to the pre-pared baking dish and sprinkle with the remaining half of the cheese. Bake for 30 to 40 minutes, or until browned.

Makes 12 Servings

Tofu and Vegetable Stir-Fry

Tofu slid slowly into our family meals, but this received applause. Here tofu transforms stir-fried vegetables into a tasty main dish.

2 teaspoons soy sauce
1 teaspoon Worcestershire sauce
½ teaspoon sesame oil
½ teaspoon grated fresh ginger
1 clove garlic, minced
½ pound firm or extra-firm tofu,
   cut into ½-inch cubes
1½ teaspoons cornstarch
½ cup water

2 tablespoons canola or olive oil
2 inner stalks celery, sliced
2 small zucchini or yellow crookneck
   squash, sliced
1 small red bell pepper, seeded and
   cut into ¾-inch squares
¼ pound small white or brown
   mushrooms, sliced
8 cherry tomatoes, halved

In a small bowl, combine the soy sauce, Worcestershire, sesame oil, ginger and garlic. Add the tofu, toss lightly and let stand for 5 minutes.

Remove the tofu from the soy mixture with a slotted spoon. Dissolve the cornstarch in the water and mix into the soy sauce mixture; set aside.

In a large skillet or wok, heat the oil over medium heat. Add the celery, zucchini and pepper and stir-fry for 2 minutes. Add the mushrooms and stir-fry for 1 minute. Stir in the reserved soy sauce mixture and cook until thickened, stirring occasionally. Add the tofu and tomatoes, heat through and serve immediately.

Makes 3 to 4 Servings

Twice-Baked Potatoes

Baked stuffed potatoes are a welcome delight. They can be done in advance and swiftly reheated. This beloved dish from my childhood always accompanied Mom's meat loaf and green beans.

6 large russet potatoes
Salt and freshly ground black pepper
  to taste
½ cup plain yogurt
1 tablespoon butter
Milk

Chopped fresh chives or green onion
  tops for accompaniment
1 cup shredded Gruyère or Jarlsberg
  cheese for accompaniment
¾ cup light-style sour cream for
  accompaniment

Preheat the oven to 425°. Prick the potatoes with a fork a few times and place them in a baking pan. Bake for about 40 minutes, or until tender. Cool for a few minutes. Reduce the oven heat to 350°.

With a knife, cut an oval from the top of each potato. With a spoon, scoop out the insides of the potato to form a shell, stopping about ¼ to ½ inch from the sides of the potato. Place the insides of the potato into a bowl. Mix in the salt, pepper, yogurt, butter and enough milk to form a fluffy mixture. Spoon the potato mixture back into the potato shells. (If desired, you can cover the potatoes at this point and chill until ready to serve).

Bake the potatoes for about 15 minutes, or until heated through. Accompany with the chives, cheese and sour cream to spoon over the top.

Makes 6 Servings

Vegetable Garden Stew

Yaya, my Greek mother-in-law, was always more lavish with the olive oil than I, on lacing this garden vegetable stew. You can change the type or proportion of vegetables here, based on your whim.

2 tablespoons olive oil
1 large red or yellow onion, chopped
2 cloves garlic, minced
3 tablespoons tomato paste
1¼ cups chicken broth
2 carrots, cut into 1-inch pieces
2 potatoes, peeled and cut into
    ½-inch strips
¾ pound green beans, cut into
    1½-inch pieces

2 zucchini, cut into ¾-inch slices
2 yellow crookneck squash, cut into
    ¾-inch slices
Salt and freshly ground black pepper
    to taste
2 tablespoons minced fresh flat-leaf
    parsley
2 tablespoons freshly grated Parmesan
    or Romano cheese

In a large pot, heat the oil over medium-high heat. Add the onion and sauté until soft, about 2 to 3 minutes. Add the garlic, tomato paste, broth, carrots and potatoes. Cover the pot and simmer for 10 minutes.

Add the beans, zucchini and crookneck squash and simmer until the squash is tender-crisp, about 5 minutes. Sprinkle with salt, pepper and parsley. Ladle the stew into bowls and sprinkle with the cheese.

Makes 4 to 5 Servings

Apricot-Olive Galette

In the nineties as I pursued pizza baking for a small cookbook, *Pizzette*, I encountered the French way for this cartwheel-shaped pie. It is even more interesting when a touch of nut flour is added to the dough. Serve this savory bread warm, cut into wedges, for an appetizer or salad accompaniment. Usually I double the recipe and slip one pie—when just baked and barely cooled—into the freezer for later.

1 package active dry yeast
½ cup lukewarm water (105° to 115°)
3 tablespoons olive oil
1 tablespoon honey
1 egg
¾ teaspoon salt
⅓ cup whole wheat flour, chestnut
   flour or pistachio flour

1⅓ cups unbleached all-purpose flour
1 tablespoon minced lemon zest
1 tablespoon minced fresh rosemary
¼ cup pitted salt-cured black olives
⅓ cup pistachio nuts
⅓ cup slivered dried apricots

In a large bowl, stir the yeast into the lukewarm warm water and let stand for about 10 minutes, until bubbly. Add 2 tablespoons of the oil with the honey, egg and salt and mix together with a wooden spoon. Add the whole wheat or nut flour and mix well. Gradually add enough of the all-purpose flour to make a soft dough. Add the lemon zest and rosemary and beat well with a heavy duty mixer or wooden spoon until the dough is smooth and elastic. Transfer the dough to a lightly oiled bowl, cover with plastic wrap and let rise until doubled in size, about 1½ hours.

Punch down the dough, transfer it to a lightly floured work surface and knead lightly. Roll out the dough (or pat out with greased fingers) into a 15-inch circle and place in a greased 14-inch pizza pan or on a baking sheet. Push the edge of the dough slightly to form a rim. Brush the dough with the remaining 1 tablespoon oil. Sprinkle the dough with the olives, nuts and apricots. Cover with a towel and let it stand in a warm place for 30 minutes to rise slightly.

Preheat the oven to 450°. Bake the galette for 6 to 8 minutes, or until golden.

Makes 1 Pizza-Sized Bread

Cheese Brioche

Over the years I have delighted in shaping this dough in myriad ways. Sometimes like a star for an appetizer party; other times done in loaves or individual buns with a top-knot. With a soup and salad, this golden cheese bread makes a meal. It is best served warm to release the buttery flavor and make the texture springy.

1 package active dry yeast	3 eggs
¼ cup lukewarm water (105° to 115°)	1 egg, separated
½ cup milk	About 3¼ cups unbleached all-purpose
6 tablespoons butter or margarine	flour
2 tablespoons sugar	1½ cups diced or shredded Gruyère,
½ teaspoon salt	Jarlsberg or Swiss-style cheese

In a small bowl or cup, stir the yeast into the lukewarm water and let stand for about 10 minutes, until bubbly. In a saucepan or in the microwave, heat the milk until lukewarm.

In a large bowl, beat the butter until creamy. Add the sugar, salt, eggs and egg yolk and beat until well mixed. Add the lukewarm milk and the yeast mixture to the bowl. Gradually add just enough flour to make a soft dough, beating well after each addition.

Transfer the dough to a lightly floured board and knead until the dough is smooth and satiny. Place the dough in a lightly oiled bowl, cover with plastic wrap and let rise in a warm place until doubled in size, about 1½ hours.

Punch down the dough and transfer it to a lightly floured board. Knead the cheese into the dough. Divide the dough into three pieces. Roll each piece into a rope about 14 inches long. Braid the dough securely, but not too tightly, on a greased baking sheet. Cover the braid with plastic wrap and let rise in a warm place until doubled in size, about 45 minutes.

Preheat the oven to 350°. Brush the bread with lightly beaten egg white and bake for 30 to 35 minutes, or until golden brown and the loaf sounds hollow when thumped.

Makes 1 Large Loaf

Breads

Rosemary Whole Wheat Loaves

I like to duck into the herb garden off the kitchen to snip several wands of fresh rosemary for this hearty bread. Mother often enhanced the whole wheat bread with hazelnuts and orange zest when I was growing up. This bread is excellent toasted and served as an appetizer, spread with chèvre and topped with sun-dried tomatoes.

2 packages active dry yeast
2½ cups lukewarm water (105° to 115°)
2 cups stone-ground whole wheat
    flour
About 3 cups unbleached all-purpose
    flour

2½ teaspoons salt
3 tablespoons honey
3 tablespoons olive oil, plus more for
    brushing
2 tablespoons chopped fresh rosemary

In a small bowl or cup, stir the yeast into ½ cup of the water and let stand for about 10 minutes, until bubbly.

In a large bowl, combine the whole wheat flour, ½ cup of the all-purpose flour and the salt. Add the remaining 2 cups water and the honey and olive oil. Mix well with a heavy-duty electric mixer or wooden spoon. Mix in the yeast mixture and 1 tablespoon of the rosemary. Add enough of the remaining flour to make a soft dough. Knead with the dough hook for 10 minutes, or transfer to a lightly floured work surface and knead by hand until the dough is smooth and elastic. Place the dough in a lightly oiled bowl, cover with plastic wrap and let rise until doubled in size, about 1½ hours.

Punch down the dough and transfer to a lightly floured work surface. Divide the dough in half and shape into 2 oval loaves. Place the loaves on a lightly greased baking sheet, cover and let rise until doubled in size, about 45 minutes.

Preheat the oven to 375°. Brush the dough with olive oil and sprinkle with the remaining 1 tablespoon rosemary. Bake the loaves for 35 minutes, or until golden brown and the loaves sound hollow when thumped. Cool on a rack.

Makes 2 Loaves

Persimmon Tea Loaves

With a persimmon tree in the garden, its brilliant fruit beckons to be picked and savored. My neighbor, Wayne Hoyer shared this fast tea bread recipe, which freezes well. I like to slice it thinly and spread it with cream cheese and minced candied ginger.

1 cup sugar
1 cup plus 2 tablespoons all-purpose
 flour
1 teaspoon baking soda
¼ teaspoon salt
1 teaspoon baking powder
1 teaspoon cinnamon
1 teaspoon ground ginger

½ teaspoon ground allspice
1 egg
1 teaspoon vanilla extract
¼ cup milk
1 cup persimmon pulp (see *Note*)
1 teaspoon butter, melted
½ cup chopped walnuts or pecans

Preheat the oven to 350°. In a bowl, combine the sugar, flour, soda, salt, baking powder, cinnamon, ginger and allspice and mix well. Add the egg and beat well. Stir in the vanilla, milk, persimmon pulp and butter. Add the flour mixture to the persimmon mixture and beat until blended. Stir in the nuts. Spoon the batter into 2 greased and floured 4-by-7-inch loaf pans. Bake for 45 to 50 minutes, or until a toothpick inserted into the center of the bread comes out clean. Cool for 10 minutes before removing the loaves from the pans.

Note: To make persimmon pulp, freeze the persimmons whole; later you can easily slip off the skin by holding the fruit under hot water for a few seconds. Once the fruit thaws, puree it in a blender.

Makes 2 Loaves

Lou's Hazelnut Rounds

My Swedish great grandparents had a bakery in Gothenberg at the turn-of-the-century, so baking is in my genes! I find bread baking great therapy and love kneading and shaping the dough. This recipe utilizes a starter to give it wonderful flavor. Plan ahead because it takes at least 6 hours to develop the starter.

Baked in 1-pound coffee cans, this delicious orange-scented nut bread slices into neat rounds for easy handling. Toast it and spread with honey for breakfast or top with an array of pestos for a blissful appetizer or sandwich—a treat shy on fat. Complementary pestos are sun-dried tomato, roasted garlic, olive, basil or thyme.

¾ cup (4 ounces) hazelnuts or walnuts
1 package active dry yeast
¼ cup lukewarm water (105° to 115°)
¼ cup honey or dark molasses
¼ cup olive, walnut or canola oil
2 teaspoons salt

Zest of 2 oranges, cut into slivers
1 cup Starter (recipe follows)
2½ cups warm water
3 cups whole wheat flour
3 to 3½ cups unbleached all-purpose
   or bread flour

Preheat the oven to 325°. Place the nuts in a baking pan and bake for 8 to 10 minutes, or until lightly toasted; cool for a few minutes. If using hazelnuts, rub them between two paper towels to remove most of the papery skins. Let the nuts cool completely and chop coarsely.

In a large bowl, stir the yeast into the lukewarm water and let stand for about 10 minutes, until bubbly. Add the honey or molasses with the oil, salt, orange zest and Starter and beat until smooth. Mix in the warm water and whole wheat flour. Gradually mix in enough of the all-purpose or bread flour to make a soft dough. Mix in the hazelnuts.

With a heavy duty mixer, knead the dough with the dough hook for about 8 to 10 minutes, or knead the dough by hand on a lightly floured work surface until the dough is smooth and satiny. Place the dough in a lightly oiled bowl, cover with plastic wrap and let rise until doubled in size, about 1½ hours.

Punch down the dough and transfer it to a lightly floured work surface. Knead the dough slightly and divide it into 5 equal pieces. Shape each dough piece into a ball and place each dough ball in a greased 1-pound coffee can.

Breads

Cover the coffee cans with a towel and let the dough rise until it has slightly more than doubled in size, about 45 minutes.

Preheat the oven to 375°. Bake the loaves for 30 minutes, or until the loaves sound hollow when thumped. Cool the loaves in the coffee cans for 5 minutes; then, remove the loaves from the pans and transfer them to a rack to cool completely.

Makes 5 Loaves

Variation: Chestnut Loaves

Omit the orange zest. Knead ½ cup chestnut flour into the dough, replacing ½ cup of the all-purpose flour. Shape the dough into 2 long, slender logs, each about 16 inches long. Place the loaves on a parchment-lined baking pan. Bake the loaves for about 35 minutes. Makes 2 loaves.

Starter

1 teaspoon active dry yeast	1 teaspoon honey
1 cup lukewarm water (105° to 115°)	2 cups unbleached all-purpose flour

In a large bowl, stir the yeast into the lukewarm water. Stir in the honey. Gradually mix in the flour, beating until smooth. Cover the bowl loosely with plastic wrap and let stand at room temperature for at least 6 hours or overnight.

Note: You can refrigerate the starter for up to 1 week before using it. After using the starter, replenish it with ½ cup warm water and 1 cup flour, mixing until smooth. Cover the replenished starter and let stand at room temperature for 2 to 3 hours; then refrigerate. Use within 1 week and replenish, or place in the freezer. Thaw frozen starter at room temperature for 3 hours before using.

Lou's Hazelnut Rounds

Breads

Sticky Caramel-Cinnamon Rolls

A beloved sweet roll for decades since childhood—a chewy caramel glaze coats the bottom of these light cinnamon rolls. I like to bake a double batch and keep the extras in the freezer.

1 package active dry yeast
¼ cup lukewarm water (105° to 115°)
½ cup milk
6½ tablespoons butter
¼ cup granulated sugar
½ teaspoon salt
1 teaspoon vanilla extract

2 eggs
3½ cups unbleached all-purpose flour
1 cup firmly packed brown sugar
¼ cup light corn syrup
1 tablespoon butter, melted
1½ teaspoons cinnamon

In a small bowl or cup, stir the yeast into the lukewarm water and let stand for about 10 minutes, until bubbly.

In a saucepan, heat the milk and 4 tablespoons of the butter until the butter melts and pour it into a large bowl. Stir in the sugar, salt and vanilla extract and let stand until the mixture is lukewarm. Stir the yeast mixture into the milk mixture. Add the eggs one at a time and beat until smooth. Gradually mix in enough of the flour to make a soft dough. Transfer the dough to a floured work surface and knead until the dough is smooth and elastic. Place the dough in a lightly oiled bowl, cover with a towel and let rise until doubled in size, about 1½ hours.

Preheat the oven to 350°. Place the remaining 2½ tablespoons of the butter, ⅔ cup of the brown sugar and the corn syrup in a 9-by-13-inch baking pan and place in the oven just until the butter melts and the mixture bubbles, about 7 minutes. Spread the mixture evenly in the pan.

Punch down the dough and transfer it to a lightly floured work surface. Roll the dough into a 10-by-12-inch rectangle. Brush the dough with the melted butter and sprinkle with the cinnamon and the remaining ⅓ cup brown sugar.

Starting from the long edge, roll up the dough securely, jelly roll-style, and cut into 1-inch slices. Place the slices in the caramel-coated pan, cover with a towel and let rise until doubled in size, about 1 hour.

Preheat the oven to 350°. Bake the rolls for 30 minutes, or until golden brown. Immediately turn the rolls upside down on a rack and lift off the pan. Serve warm or at room temperature.

Makes 1 Dozen

Sticky Caramel-Cinnamon Rolls

Breads

Chocolate Streusel Twist

This decorative coffee bread has a striking pinwheel design that is easy to master. It has graced our family breakfast table on Easter and Christmas since the sixties.

1 package active dry yeast
¼ cup lukewarm water (105° to 115°)
6 tablespoons sugar
6 tablespoons butter
1 teaspoon salt
2 teaspoons vanilla extract
3 eggs
About 4½ cups unbleached all-purpose flour

1 cup warm milk
½ cup sugar
3 tablespoons flour
3 tablespoons butter, softened
2 tablespoons unsweetened cocoa powder
½ teaspoon cinnamon
1 egg white, beaten until foamy
¼ cup sliced almonds

In a large bowl, stir the yeast into the lukewarm water and let stand for about 10 minutes, until bubbly.

Add the 6 tablespoons sugar, 6 tablespoons butter, salt, vanilla extract and eggs to the bowl and beat well. Add 1 cup of the flour and beat until smooth. Add the milk and gradually add 2 more cups of the flour, beating well. Gradually add enough of the remaining 1 cup of the flour to make a soft dough.

Transfer the dough to a lightly floured work surface and knead lightly. Place the dough in a lightly oiled bowl, cover with plastic wrap and let rise in a warm place until doubled in size, about 1½ hours.

In a small bowl, mix together the ½ cup sugar, 3 tablespoons flour, softened butter, cocoa powder and cinnamon; set aside.

Punch down the dough, transfer to a lightly floured work surface and knead lightly. Cut the dough in half. Roll one dough half into a 10-by-4-inch rectangle and spread with half of the cocoa mixture.

Starting from the long edge, roll up the dough securely, jelly roll-style, and place seam-side down on a buttered or parchment-lined baking sheet. Repeat the filling and rolling process with the remaining dough and cocoa mixture.

Cut the rolls at ¾-inch intervals part of the way through the dough, to within ½ inch of the bottom.

Alternately, on opposite sides, pull and twist each dough slice to lay flat, beginning at one end of each roll. Cover the dough with a towel and let rise in a warm place until doubled in size, about 45 minutes.

Preheat the oven to 350°. Brush the dough with the beaten egg white and sprinkle with the nuts. Place the breads in the oven, reduce the oven heat to 325° and bake for 30 to 35 minutes, or until golden brown.

Makes 2 Loaves

Chocolate Streusel Twist

Breads

Dutch Baby

This was a house classic in the fifties. A jaunty puffy oven pancake delighted family or guests for a weekend brunch. A choice of toppings—berries, yogurt, sour cream, fluffy honey butter—lended flair.

2 tablespoons butter
4 eggs
1 cup milk
1 cup all-purpose flour
1 tablespoon grated lemon zest,
   or ⅛ teaspoon nutmeg

Fresh strawberries, raspberries and/or
   blueberries for accompaniments
Plain yogurt, sour cream or
   Whipped Honey Butter (recipe
   follows) for accompaniments

Preheat the oven to 425°. Place the butter in a 10-inch round baking pan and heat in the oven until melted, about 5 minutes.

With a blender or food processor, mix the eggs, milk, flour and lemon zest or nutmeg until smooth. Pour the batter into the hot pan and bake for 20 to 25 minutes, or until puffed and golden brown.

Cut the Dutch Baby into wedges and serve topped with berries, yogurt, sour cream or Whipped Honey Butter.

Whipped Honey Butter

6 tablespoons unsalted butter, softened   6 tablespoons honey

With an electric mixer, beat the butter until creamy. Add the honey and beat until thick, light and fluffy. Makes about ¾ cup.

Makes 4 Servings

Breads

Kingsley House Granola

This is my house granola, named for the street corner. This is a wonderful high fiber low-fat cereal that is great in a smoothie for breakfast. I like to puree my morning drink with ½ cup yogurt, 1 diced fresh navel orange from the garden, ½ frozen banana, cut into chunks, and ½ cup frozen strawberries or diced mango. I peel the bananas and cut them in half before freezing in a locking plastic bag, so each half is ready for a smoothie. I often bake two batches of granola at once, as it keeps well in a tin. Varying the nuts and flakes each baking lends variety to the day.

½ cup apple juice or orange juice
2 tablespoons honey
1½ teaspoons walnut, sesame or
   olive oil
1½ teaspoons cinnamon
½ teaspoon ground coriander
¼ teaspoon freshly ground nutmeg
¼ teaspoon salt
2 teaspoons vanilla extract

Zest of 1 orange, slivered
2 cups old-fashioned rolled oats,
   or use part barley flakes
1½ cups wheat bran
⅓ cup chopped walnuts, pistachio
   nuts or lightly toasted skinned
   hazelnuts
⅓ cup chopped dried apricots or dried
   cherries (optional)

Preheat the oven to 325°. In a small saucepan, combine the apple or orange juice, honey, oil, cinnamon, coriander, nutmeg and salt. Heat over medium heat until hot. Stir in the vanilla extract and orange zest.

Place the oats, bran and nuts in a large bowl, pour the juice mixture over the top and mix well. Spread the mixture in an oiled 10-by-15-inch baking pan and bake for 20 minutes. Reduce the oven heat to 300° and bake for 10 minutes longer, or until the mixture is lightly toasted.

Remove the mixture from the oven and stir in the apricots or cherries, if using. Cool the granola and store it in a tightly closed container.

Note: If you double the recipe, bake it in two pans.

Makes 4 Cups

Breads

Triple Ginger Cookies

As ginger has come into vogue in the past decade, I utilize its spicy heat in three forms to tantalize the palate in this crispy caramel cookie wafer.

½ cup cold unsalted butter,
   cut into pieces
½ cup dark brown sugar, packed
1 tablespoon finely minced fresh
   ginger
1 tablespoon ground ginger
½ teaspoon vanilla extract

1 cup plus 2 tablespoons bleached
   all-purpose flour
¼ teaspoon baking soda
Dash salt
⅓ cup finely diced crystallized ginger
   (about ⅛-inch bits)

Preheat the oven to 350°. With an electric mixer, mix the butter and sugar until smooth and creamy. Add the fresh ginger, ground ginger, vanilla, flour, soda and salt and mix just until the dough comes together. Transfer the dough to a large sheet of waxed paper and form into a 1½-inch cylinder. Wrap the dough in plastic wrap and chill until firm.

Cut the dough into thin slices and place the slices on a parchment-lined or lightly greased baking sheet. Sprinkle with crystallized ginger and bake for 6 to 8 minutes, or until browned.

Makes 4 dozen

Bittersweet Chocolate Hazelnut Cookies

The favorite Toll House cookie gets an uplift with hazelnuts and hand-chopped slivers of chocolate. I also like to substitute ¼ cup of nut flour—hazelnut, almond or pistachio—for some of the all-purpose flour specified.

½ cup butter
½ cup granulated sugar
½ cup brown sugar, packed
½ teaspoon vanilla extract
1 egg
1⅛ cups all-purpose flour

½ teaspoon baking soda
½ teaspoon salt
6 ounces bittersweet chocolate, chopped
½ cup chopped toasted hazelnuts, almonds, walnuts or pecans

Preheat the oven to 375°. With an electric mixer, mix the butter and sugars until smooth and creamy. Mix in the vanilla and egg.

In a bowl, stir together the flour, baking soda and salt. Add the flour mixture to the butter mixture, mixing until blended. Mix in the chocolate and nuts. Drop tablespoons of the dough onto a greased baking sheet. Bake for 8 to 10 minutes, or until golden brown.

Note: These are excellent with dried cherries and pistachios replacing the chocolate and hazelnuts.

Makes 2½ dozen

Pistachio Nut Brownies

Since 4-H days I've baked this winning brownie recipe. Recently it needed an update when I was tripling a batch for a party. Fashionable pistachios filled the role as a stand-in for traditional walnuts. This large-scale recipe is ideal when I need a quantity of cookies for an event. If you wish, cut the baked panful into large squares to serve as cake with a scoop of coffee or vanilla bean ice cream.

6 ounces bittersweet chocolate,
  chopped
1 cup unsalted butter
1¼ cups all-purpose flour
⅔ cup unsweetened cocoa powder
1½ teaspoons baking powder

¼ teaspoon salt
6 eggs
2¼ cups sugar
2 teaspoons vanilla extract
¾ cup raw pistachio nuts

Preheat the oven to 350°. Line a 10-by-15-inch baking pan with foil, shiny side up, and grease the foil lightly. In the top of a double boiler, melt the chocolate with the butter over hot water; stir until blended and cool the mixture.

In a bowl, mix together the flour, cocoa, baking powder and salt. In another bowl, beat the eggs with a wire whisk or electric mixer. Add the sugar and vanilla extract and beat until thick and light in color. Stir in the chocolate mixture and dry ingredients. Spread the batter evenly in the prepared pan and sprinkle with the nuts. Bake for 25 to 30 minutes, or until set (do not overbake). Cool the brownies and cut into squares.

Makes 5 dozen

Lemon Cheese Tart

My cooking class students claim this is one of their favorite recipes for reproducing at home. The crust is easy for any novice to make. I shared the recipe with the Palo Alto Junior League for their "Private Collection" cookbook.

1 cup all-purpose flour
6 tablespoons butter
2 tablespoons confectioners' sugar
8 ounces low-fat or regular cream
  cheese
¾ cup granulated sugar

3 eggs
2 teaspoons grated lemon zest
½ cup lemon juice
Mint sprigs, sliced kiwi fruit or
  blueberries for garnish

Preheat the oven to 425°. With a food processor, mix together the flour, butter and confectioners' sugar until it forms a crumbly mixture. Pat the mixture into the bottom and up the sides of an 11-inch flan pan with scalloped sides and a removable bottom. Place the pan in the freezer for 10 minutes. Bake the tart shell for 8 to 10 minutes, or until lightly browned; cool completely. Reduce the oven heat to 350°.

With an electric mixer, beat the cream cheese until smooth and creamy. Add the granulated sugar, eggs, lemon zest and lemon juice and beat well. Pour the mixture into the butter tart shell and spread the top evenly. Bake for 20 minutes, or until the center is set. Cool the tart completely and chill until serving time. Cut the tart into wedges and garnish with mint sprigs or fruit.

Makes 8 Servings

Desserts

Strawberry and Whipped Cream Cheese Tart

This party tart goes together in a flash. It is a favorite of mine from the fifties when I was a home economist at *Sunset* magazine. For the holiday season, I like to wreath the top with strawberries and sliced kiwi fruit. Blueberries also make a lovely tart.

1 cup all-purpose flour
6 tablespoons butter
2 tablespoons confectioners' sugar
3 ounces low-fat or regular
   cream cheese
¼ cup confectioners' sugar

2 tablespoons Grand Marnier, curaçao,
Triple Sec or framboise liqueur
1 cup heavy cream
1 pint fresh strawberries, hulled,
   halved or sliced if large

Preheat the oven to 425°. With a food processor, mix together the flour, butter and 2 tablespoons confectioners' sugar until it forms a crumbly mixture. Pat the mixture into the bottom and up the sides of an 11-inch flan pan with scalloped sides and a removable bottom. Place the pan in the freezer for 10 minutes. Bake the tart shell for 8 to 10 minutes, or until lightly browned; cool completely. Reduce the oven heat to 350°.

With a wire whisk or electric mixer, beat the cream cheese with the ¼ cup confectioners' sugar until light and fluffy. Add the liqueur and mix well. Add the cream and whip until light and fluffy. Pour the mixture into the tart shell and spread the top evenly.

Top with the strawberries in a decorative pattern. Cut the tart into wedges to serve.

Makes 8 Servings

Swedish Nut Cake

This feathery light cake with a broiled coconut frosting sometimes goes by the name of Lazy Daisy Cake. It is one of the quick cakes of the thirties that Mother used to whip up in the Hobart commercial mixer, just before dinner.

½ cup milk
3 tablespoons butter
3 eggs
1 cup sugar
1 cup all-purpose flour
1 teaspoon baking powder
½ teaspoon salt
1 teaspoon vanilla extract

Coconut-Caramel Topping

3 tablespoons butter
2 tablespoons heavy cream or melted vanilla ice cream
½ cup brown sugar, packed
½ cup shredded coconut
½ cup chopped pecans

Preheat the oven to 350°. Prepare a 9-inch square cake pan by lining it with parchment paper or greasing and flouring it. In a saucepan, bring the milk and butter to a boil; remove the pan from the heat and set aside. In a large bowl, beat the eggs until thick. Add the sugar and beat until the mixture turns pale in color.

In another bowl, stir together the flour, baking powder and salt. Add the flour mixture to the egg mixture and mix well. Carefully stir in the hot milk mixture and vanilla extract and mix well. Immediately pour the mixture into the prepared cake pan and bake for 30 minutes, or until the top springs back when touched with a finger.

To Prepare the Coconut-Caramel Topping: Preheat the broiler. In a saucepan, combine the butter, cream or ice cream and brown sugar. Cook over medium heat until the mixture begins to bubble, stirring until blended. Stir in the coconut and nuts. Spread the topping on the cake and place under the broiler until it bubbles, about 1 minute; cool. Cut into squares to serve.

Makes 12 Servings

Desserts

Chocolate Fudge Birthday Cake with Seven-Minute Frosting

Hamburgers, root beer floats and this wonderful chocolate cake always graced my friend, Sally Snideler's birthday table while I was growing up in Oregon. Serve it at your next birthday celebration or other family occasion.

½ cup butter
½ cup brown sugar, packed
1½ cups granulated sugar
2 eggs
2 cups all-purpose flour
½ teaspoon salt
1 teaspoon baking soda
1 teaspoon baking powder
1 cup buttermilk

⅓ cup hot water
½ cup unsweetened cocoa powder

Seven-Minute Frosting
¼ cup water
¾ cup sugar
½ teaspoon cream of tartar
⅛ teaspoon salt
2 egg whites

Preheat the oven to 350°. Line two 9-inch round cake pans with parchment or grease and flour the pans. With an electric mixer, mix the butter and sugars until light and fluffy. Add the eggs and beat until smooth.

In a bowl, stir together the flour, salt, baking soda and baking powder. Add the dry ingredients to the butter mixture alternately with the buttermilk and mix well.

In a bowl, stir the hot water into the cocoa and mix until smooth. Add the cocoa mixture to the cake batter and beat until well mixed.

Pour the batter into the prepared pans and bake for 25 to 30 minutes, or until a toothpick inserted into the center comes out clean. Cool the cakes for 10 minutes. Invert the pans onto a rack and peel off the paper, if using. Cool the cakes completely.

To make the Seven-Minute Frosting: In the top of a double boiler, combine the water, sugar, cream of tartar, salt and egg whites. Cook over simmering water, beating with an electric mixer or rotary beater until the frosting stands in peaks, about 7 minutes.

To Assemble the Cake: Place one cake layer on a serving platter and spread the top with a layer of Seven Minute Frosting. Top with the second cake layer, aligning the edges. Frost the top of and sides of the cake with frosting.

To serve, cut the cake into wedges.

Makes 12 Servings

Chocolate Fudge Birthday Cake with Seven-Minute Frosting

Desserts

Chocolate-Mint Roll

This luscious chocolate sponge roll annually graced the holiday table at home on Christmas day. The refreshing mint flavor lends an ambrosial taste treat to the feathery chocolate cake. As an alternate topping instead of the glaze, ribbon the surface with whipped cream and shower with bittersweet chocolate curls or shavings.

¼ cup unsweetened cocoa powder
1¼ cups unsifted confectioners' sugar,
   plus more as needed
1 tablespoon all-purpose flour
⅛ teaspoon salt
6 eggs, separated
¼ teaspoon cream of tartar
1 teaspoon vanilla extract
1 cup heavy cream
2 tablespoons crème de menthe, rum
   or Cointreau

Chocolate Glaze
2 ounces semisweet chocolate,
   chopped
1½ tablespoons butter
¼ cup light cream or brewed coffee
⅓ cup confectioners' sugar

Preheat the oven to 400°. Sift the cocoa, 1 cup of the sugar, the flour and salt into a bowl. In a clean, oil-free bowl, beat the egg whites until foamy. Add the cream of tartar and beat until soft peaks form. Add the remaining ¼ cup of the confectioners' sugar and beat until stiff peaks form.

In another bowl, beat the egg yolks until thick and lemon colored. Mix in the vanilla extract and the cocoa mixture. Add ¼ of the egg white mixture to the egg yolk mixture and fold in until lightened. Carefully fold in the remaining egg white mixture until incorporated.

Grease a 10-by-15-inch baking pan and line it with parchment or waxed paper. Spread the batter evenly in the prepared pan and bake for 10 minutes, or until the top springs back when touched lightly with a finger. Immediately invert the cake onto a towel dusted with confectioners' sugar; remove the pan and peel off the paper.

To Assemble the Cake: Starting from the short edges, roll up the cake with the towel, jelly roll-style, and cool completely.

Whip the heavy cream until soft peaks form. Add the liqueur and confectioners' sugar to taste, about 1 tablespoon, and whip until blended.

Unroll the cake and spread with the whipped cream. Reroll the cake without the towel, and chill completely.

To Prepare the Chocolate Glaze: Melt the chocolate with the butter in a saucepan. Add the cream or coffee and stir until blended. Remove the saucepan from the heat and beat in the confectioners' sugar. Cool the mixture until slightly thickened and spread on top of the cake to resemble bark on a tree branch.

To serve, cut the cake diagonally into serving pieces.

Makes 8 Servings

Chocolate-Mint Roll

Hazelnut Chocolate Torte

This ethereal nut sponge cake is lovely with raspberries and ice cream. Growing up in Oregon, hazelnuts were the house nut.

6 ounces bittersweet or semisweet chocolate
1 cup toasted skinned hazelnuts (see page 112)
1 tablespoon minced orange zest
5 eggs, separated
⅛ teaspoon salt
⅛ teaspoon cream of tartar

⅔ cup sugar
1 teaspoon vanilla extract
¼ teaspoon almond extract
3 tablespoons cake flour
About 1½ cups fresh raspberries (optional)
Whipped cream or ice cream for accompaniment

Preheat the oven to 350°. With a food processor or blender, process the chocolate until finely chopped; transfer the chopped chocolate to a bowl. Add the nuts to the food processor or blender and process until finely ground. Add the orange zest and process until just mixed. Transfer the mixture to the bowl with the chocolate.

In a clean, oil-free bowl, beat the egg whites until foamy. Add the salt and cream of tartar and beat until soft peaks form. Add 3 tablespoons of the sugar and beat until stiff, glossy peaks form.

In another bowl, beat the egg yolks until thick and lemon-colored. Add the remaining sugar and the vanilla and almond extracts, beating until thick and pale in color. Add the nut-chocolate mixture and mix well. Fold ⅓ of the egg white mixture into the egg yolk mixture to lighten; then, carefully fold in the flour and the remaining egg white mixture.

Line a 9-inch springform pan with parchment paper and pour in the batter. Bake the torte for 30 to 35 minutes, or until the top springs back when pressed lightly with a finger; cool.

To serve, remove the sides of the springform and cut the torte into wedges. Accompany servings with berries, if desired, and whipped cream or ice cream.

Makes 10 Servings

Triple Orange Sponge Cake

As a child, birthday celebrations most often featured this light, tender treat. Today I like this foolproof cake, ideal for many occasions, adorned with fresh strawberries and whipped cream or with just a light coating of frosting. of frosting.

1¼ cups cake flour
1½ cups sugar
½ teaspoon salt
½ teaspoon baking powder
6 eggs, separated
1 teaspoon cream of tartar
¼ cup orange juice
1 teaspoon vanilla extract

Orange Frosting

3 tablespoons butter
2 cups confectioners' sugar
1 tablespoon orange juice concentrate
   mixed with 2 tablespoons water
1 teaspoon grated orange zest

Preheat the oven to 325°. In a bowl, combine the flour, 1 cup of the sugar, the salt and baking powder and stir to blend.

In a large, clean, oil-free bowl, beat the egg whites and cream of tartar until soft peaks begin to form. Slowly add the remaining ½ cup of the sugar and beat until stiff upright peaks form.

Make a well in the center of the flour mixture and add the egg yolks, orange juice and vanilla. With an electric mixer, beat on medium speed for 1 minute, scraping down the sides of the bowl often. Fold about ¼ of the egg white mixture into the egg yolk mixture to lighten it. Carefully fold in the remaining egg white mixture until incorporated. Pour the mixture to a 10-inch tube pan and bake for 50 minutes, or until a toothpick inserted into the center of the cake comes out clean. Invert the pan and cool the cake. Remove the cooled cake from the pan.

To Prepare the Orange Frosting: Place the frosting ingredients in a bowl and mix with an electric mixture until light, fluffy and well blended.

Place the cooled cake on a serving platter and spread evenly with the frosting. Let the frosting stand for a few minutes to set. Cut the cake into wedges to serve.

Makes 12 Servings

Desserts

Dark Chocolate Almond Cake

This luscious chocolate cake is my all-time favorite for adult birthday celebrations. It is best to bake it so the center is still moist and just barely set.

½ cup unsalted butter

8 ounces bittersweet or semisweet chocolate, chopped

6 eggs, separated

⅛ teaspoon salt

⅛ teaspoon cream of tartar

¾ cup sugar

2 tablespoons brewed coffee, Grand Marnier, Triple Sec or rum

½ cup finely ground toasted almonds or toasted skinned hazelnuts (see page 112)

6 tablespoons all-purpose flour

Dark Chocolate Glaze (Optional)

2 ounces unsweetened chocolate, chopped

2 ounces bittersweet or semisweet chocolate, chopped

¼ cup unsalted butter

Preheat the oven to 350°. Line a 9-inch springform pan with parchment paper. In the top of a double boiler, melt the butter with the chocolate over hot water and stir to blend; cool.

In a large, clean, oil-free bowl, beat the egg whites until foamy. Add the salt and cream of tartar and beat until soft peaks form. Add 3 tablespoons of the sugar and beat until stiff, glossy peaks form.

In another bowl, beat the egg yolks until thick and lemon-colored. Add the remaining sugar and the coffee or liqueur and mix well. Stir in the chocolate mixture. Fold one-third of the egg whites into the chocolate mixture to lighten it. Carefully fold in the nuts, flour and remaining egg whites until incorporated. Pour the batter into the prepared pan and smooth the top. Bake for 35 minutes, or until the center is just barely set. Cool the cake for 30 minutes.

Invert a serving plate on top of the cake pan and invert the cake onto the plate. Remove the sides of the springform and carefully peel off the parchment paper. Cool the cake to room temperature.

To Prepare the Dark Chocolate Glaze: Melt both chocolates with the butter in the top of a double boiler over simmering water, stirring to blend. Cool the glaze over ice for about 1 minute, until it just begins to thicken. Pour the glaze onto the center of the cake and quickly tip the cake so that the glaze covers the entire surface. With a cake spatula, spread the glaze over the sides of the cake.

Makes 10 to 12 Servings

Dark Chocolate Almond Cake

Bittersweet Chocolate Soufflé

Le Soufflé is a charming restaurant on the Right Bank of the Seine River in Paris where I've sampled a bevy of airy confections. This recipe always brings back memories of the ethereal creations there. It can be assembled in advance and refrigerated up to a day before baking. Extend the baking time if it is chilled.

Softened butter
⅔ cup sugar, plus more for dusting
6 ounces bittersweet or dark chocolate, chopped
6 eggs, separated
⅛ teaspoon salt

½ teaspoon cream of tartar
1 teaspoon vanilla extract, or
    1 tablespoon rum
Whipped cream, sweetened to taste, for garnish

Coat a 1½-quart soufflé dish, 10-inch round baking dish, or eight 8-ounce individual soufflé dishes with butter and dust all sides with sugar.

In a small bowl, heat the chocolate in a microwave on medium (50%) power or in a double boiler over hot water until melted; cool slightly.

In a large, clean, oil-free bowl, beat the egg whites until foamy. Add the salt and cream of tartar and beat until soft peaks form. Add 3 tablespoons of the sugar and beat until stiff peaks form, but are not dry.

In another bowl, beat the egg yolks until thick and lemon-colored. Add the remaining sugar and the vanilla or rum and beat well. Stir in the melted chocolate mixture. Fold one-fourth of the egg whites into the chocolate mixture to lighten it. Carefully fold in the remaining egg whites until incorporated.

Spoon the soufflé mixture into the prepared baking dish or dishes.

Preheat the oven to 375° for 1 large soufflé or 400° for individual soufflés. Bake the large soufflé for 30 to 35 minutes, or the individual soufflés for 10 to 12 minutes, or until the center is set. Serve portions garnished with sweetened whipped cream.

Makes 6 to 8 Servings

Frozen Grand Marnier Soufflé

Dining on the sun-swept terrace of the Danieli Royal Excelsior above the Grand Canal in Venice in the sixties, I was awestruck as the waiter toted out frozen Grand Marnier soufflés to our party of food editors. I determined to recreate this masterpiece and have cherished it ever since.

¾ cup sugar
¼ cup water
2 eggs
1 cup heavy cream

2 tablespoons orange juice concentrate
3 tablespoons Grand Marnier
2 tablespoons grated orange zest
Vanilla bean ice cream (optional)

Combine the sugar and water in a saucepan and bring to a boil over high heat. Reduce the heat slightly and simmer the mixture until it reads 238° on a candy thermometer.

In a large bowl, beat the eggs until light with an electric mixer. Slowly pour in the hot sugar syrup, beating continuously until the mixture cools to room temperature.

In another bowl, whip the cream until stiff peaks form and beat in the orange juice concentrate, Grand Marnier and orange zest. Add the egg mixture to the cream mixture and gently fold the ingredients together until incorporated. Spoon the mixture into soufflé dishes or a serving container, cover and freeze until firm.

Serve the soufflé alone or pair it with vanilla bean ice cream.

Makes 6 Servings

Desserts

Danish Crème Caramel

On a first trip to Europe I indulged in this triple cream concoction in a country restaurant in suburban Copenhagen. It mingles crème caramel, caramel whipped cream and ice cream. Sublime!

1 cup sugar	1 teaspoon vanilla extract
1 pint half-and-half	1 cup heavy cream
2 cups milk	2 tablespoons rum
6 eggs	1 quart French vanilla ice cream

Preheat the oven to 350°. Heat ½ cup of the sugar in a heavy saucepan until it melts and caramelizes, shaking the pan frequently. Immediately pour the caramel into a 1½-quart ring mold and tilt the mold to coat all sides with the caramel.

In the saucepan used to make the caramel, bring the half-and-half and milk to just under the boiling point and remove from the heat. In a bowl, beat the eggs until light. Add the remaining ½ cup sugar and beat well. Stir in the hot milk and vanilla. Pour the egg-milk mixture into the caramel-lined mold and bake for 50 minutes, or until the custard is set. Cool to room temperature and refrigerate until completely chilled.

With a sharp-pointed knife, loosen the custard from the edges of the mold and invert it onto a large round platter. Holding the mold in place, quickly tilt the platter and pour off the caramel syrup into a bowl and reserve it separately. Unmold the custard and chill until serving time. Add 2 tablespoons water to the mold and heat it quickly on the stovetop to dissolve any remaining caramel; add the dissolved caramel to the reserved caramel and chill until serving time.

In a bowl, whip the cream until stiff peaks form. Add the rum and ⅓ cup of the reserved caramel syrup, mix well and transfer to a bowl. Serve wedges of custard with scoops of ice cream and a dollop of caramel whipped cream. Pass the reserved caramel syrup.

Makes 8 Servings

Sticky Hot Fudge Sundaes

Blum's and Edy's ice cream fountains were favored rendezvous for hot fudge sundaes in the fifties. When they closed, I recreated their style at home. This luscious fudge sauce sets up as it hits the cool ice cream for a rich sundae topping. It is delicious on coffee, toasted almond or vanilla bean ice cream.

6 ounces bittersweet or semisweet
   chocolate, chopped
½ cup light cream
¼ cup corn syrup

1 teaspoon vanilla extract
1 quart coffee, toasted almond or
   vanilla bean ice cream

In the top of a double boiler, heat the chocolate, cream and corn syrup over simmering water, stirring until the chocolate is melted and the mixture is smooth. Remove from the heat and stir in the vanilla extract.

Scoop portions of ice cream into dessert bowls and top with the hot fudge sauce.

Makes 8 Servings